EYEWITNESS
NATIONAL PARKS

Loggerhead turtle

Red salamander

Senior Editor Sreshtha Bhattacharya
Senior Art Editor Vikas Chauhan
Editors Bipasha Roy, Bharti Bedi, Deeksha Micek
Art Editor Noopur Dalal
Assistant Art Editor Prateek Maurya
US Editor Jennette ElNaggar
US Executive Editor Lori Cates Hand
Picture Researcher Geetika Bhandari
Picture Research Manager Taiyaba Khatoon
Senior Cartographer Mohammad Hassan
Cartographer Ashif
Manager Cartography Suresh Kumar
Managing Editor Kingshuk Ghoshal
Managing Art Editor Govind Mittal
DTP Designers Pawan Kumar, Deepak Mittal, Vikram Singh
Production Editor Shanker Prasad
Pre-production manager Balwant Singh
Production Manager Pankaj Sharma
Production Controller Laura Andrews
Jacket Designer Juhi Sheth
Senior Jackets Coordinator Priyanka Sharma Saddi
Jacket Design Development Manager Sophia MTT
DK India Editorial Head Glenda Fernandes
DK India Design Head Malavika Talukder
Publisher Andrew Macintyre
Associate Publishing Director Liz Wheeler
Art Director Karen Self
Publishing Director Jonathan Metcalf

Consultants Andrea Lankford, Stefanie Payne
Written by Andrea Mills
Authenticity readers Timothy Topper, MEd, Amber Williams

This Eyewitness Book® has been conceived by Dorling Kindersley Limited and Editions Gallimard

First American Edition, 2023
Published in the United States by DK Publishing
1745 Broadway, 20th Floor, New York, NY 10019

A catalog record for this book is available from the Library of Congress.
ISBN 978-0-7440-6973-0 (Paperback)
ISBN 978-0-7440-6974-7 (ALB)

DK books are available at special discounts when purchased in bulk for sales promotions, premiums, fund-raising, or educational use. For details, contact: DK Publishing Special Markets, 1745 Broadway, 20th Floor, New York, NY 10019
SpecialSales@dk.com

Printed and bound in China

For the curious
www.dk.com

MIX
Paper | Supporting responsible forestry
FSC™ C018179

This book was made with Forest Stewardship Council™ certified paper—one small step in DK's commitment to a sustainable future. For more information, go to **www.dk.com/our-green-pledge**.

Safety

Visitors to the national parks should follow park safety guidelines when participating in any of the outdoor activities given in this book. They must also come prepared. Here is a checklist of all the essentials necessary to stay safe while exploring the parks. Some of these items may need to be handled under the supervision of an adult.

Navigation
Plan the route and take a map or compass.

Protective layers
Bring gloves and raincoats.

Drinking water
Take a plentiful supply of water.

Food
Pack snacks to stave off hunger pangs.

Lights
Bring a flashlight and spare batteries.

First Aid
Take a First-Aid kit to deal with illness or injury.

Fire
Carry a lighter or matches for warmth.

Emergency Shelter
Pack a pop-up tent.

National Park Map

In this book, each national park is shown on a map. On it, you will be able to find a lot of information about the park, including where to enter the park, which roads and trails to take, and which natural wonders to see. The key below lists some important features in each map.

▲ Glacier

▲ Mountain, Cliff, Volcano

〰 River, Stream, Creek

···· Trail

— Road

☐ Human-made structure

— Park boundary

↑ North pointer

0 km ____ 5
0 miles ____ 5 Map scale

0 km ____ 10
0 miles ____ 10

Carbon River
Mather Memorial Parkway
N
▲ Carbon Glacier
Mount Rainier ▲
▲ Emmons Glacier
▲ Paradise Glacier
☐ **Henry M Jackson Memorial Visitor Center**
Reflection Lakes
Nisqually River
Narada Falls
Stevens Canyon Road
☐ **Ohanapecosh Visitor Center**

Map of Mount Rainier National Park

Animals in the park

National parks are great places to see wild animals in their natural environment. In this book, you will find an animal box next to each park map. It lists some of the animals found in the park. The following example shows some animals seen in Biscayne National Park.

 Manatee
 Hermit crab
 Spiny lobster
 Atlantic bottlenose dolphin

Contents

Nēnē

What is a National Park?

The US is home to 63 beautiful national parks. A national park is a region protected by the government for its treasures, including its natural wonders, incredible wildlife, and cultural heritage. In the early 20th century, a government agency called the National Park Service (NPS) was formed to safeguard these parks for all to enjoy.

Preservation and recreation

The national parks preserve the plants and animals of wild habitats and maintain ecosystems. They also protect ancient archaeological sites and important historical monuments for the future. Visitors are able to enjoy the breathtaking beauty of these vast expanses and participate in a range of recreational activities.

Stephen Mather is shown on the Mather Memorial Plaque at Zion National Park.

Founding the NPS

Many people, including early presidents and conservationists such as John Muir, campaigned for the preservation of America's wilderness. In 1916, the government created the NPS to manage the national parks. Conservationist Stephen Mather was its first director.

A WALK IN THE PARK

Natural wonders
Outstanding scenery lies at the heart of all the parks. They are packed with varied landscapes, including forests, mountains, and volcanoes.

Hikes and trails
Exploring the parks on foot, whether hiking up a trail or climbing a cliffside, can be a great way of enjoying the beauty of nature.

Historic past
Many parks pay homage to Indigenous cultures that have made their mark on the land by highlighting ancient art and local legends.

Park people

A number of people work hard to maintain, run, and preserve each national park. Park rangers protect and restore habitats, keep park visitors safe, and teach classes; naturalists run conservation projects; firefighters tackle forest fires; and builders create and repair trails, roads, and buildings. There are also many volunteers who help in maintaining the parks.

Park rangers repair stone stairs at Zion National Park.

Lands lost

As the government set up national parks, it often forced Indigenous peoples off their land. Today, the NPS is working with Indigenous communities to preserve their way of life and highlight the history and culture of their ancestral homelands within the parks through educational programs created for visitors.

The humpback whale can grow to 50 ft (15 m) long.

Parks for all

The NPS encourages everyone to visit. Free park passes are available for fourth grade schoolchildren to enjoy the great outdoors. Also, many parks are being adapted to make them more easily accessible for people with disabilities.

Wonderful wildlife
Thousands of animals inhabit the parks, including many unique and endangered species. The humpback whale is found in the waters of Glacier Bay and Channel Islands national parks.

Park plants
A spectacular array of plants grow in the parks. The Hawaiʻi silversword thrives in Hawaiʻi Volcanoes National Park and Haleakalā National Park.

US National Parks

Spanning 30 states and two territories, the 63 national parks cover nearly 84.9 million acres (34.4 million ha) of land—nearly 3.6 percent of the US—as well as adjoining waters. You will see nearly every type of habitat in these parks—from sizzling deserts and craggy mountains to icy oceans!

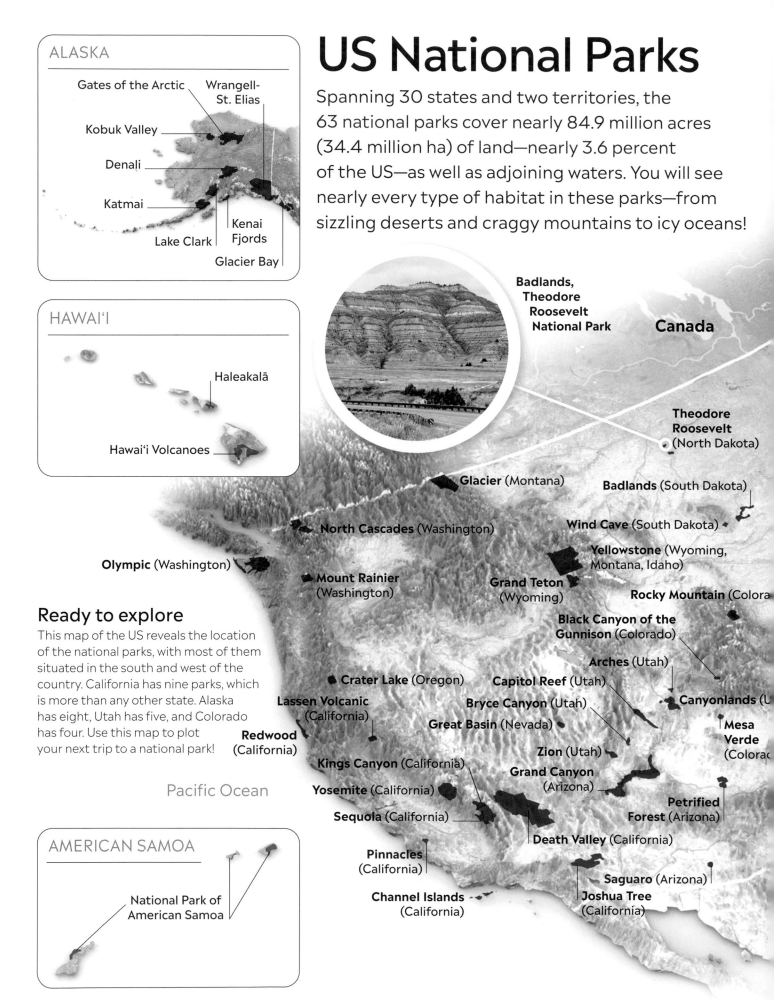

ALASKA

- Gates of the Arctic
- Wrangell-St. Elias
- Kobuk Valley
- Denali
- Katmai
- Lake Clark
- Kenai Fjords
- Glacier Bay

HAWAI'I

- Haleakalā
- Hawai'i Volcanoes

AMERICAN SAMOA

- National Park of American Samoa

Ready to explore

This map of the US reveals the location of the national parks, with most of them situated in the south and west of the country. California has nine parks, which is more than any other state. Alaska has eight, Utah has five, and Colorado has four. Use this map to plot your next trip to a national park!

Pacific Ocean

Badlands, Theodore Roosevelt National Park

Canada

Theodore Roosevelt (North Dakota)

Glacier (Montana)

Badlands (South Dakota)

North Cascades (Washington)

Wind Cave (South Dakota)

Yellowstone (Wyoming, Montana, Idaho)

Olympic (Washington)

Mount Rainier (Washington)

Grand Teton (Wyoming)

Rocky Mountain (Colora

Black Canyon of the Gunnison (Colorado)

Arches (Utah)

Crater Lake (Oregon)

Capitol Reef (Utah)

Canyonlands (U

Lassen Volcanic (California)

Bryce Canyon (Utah)

Great Basin (Nevada)

Mesa Verde (Colorad

Redwood (California)

Zion (Utah)

Kings Canyon (California)

Grand Canyon (Arizona)

Yosemite (California)

Petrified Forest (Arizona)

Sequoia (California)

Death Valley (California)

Pinnacles (California)

Saguaro (Arizona)

Joshua Tree (California)

Channel Islands (California)

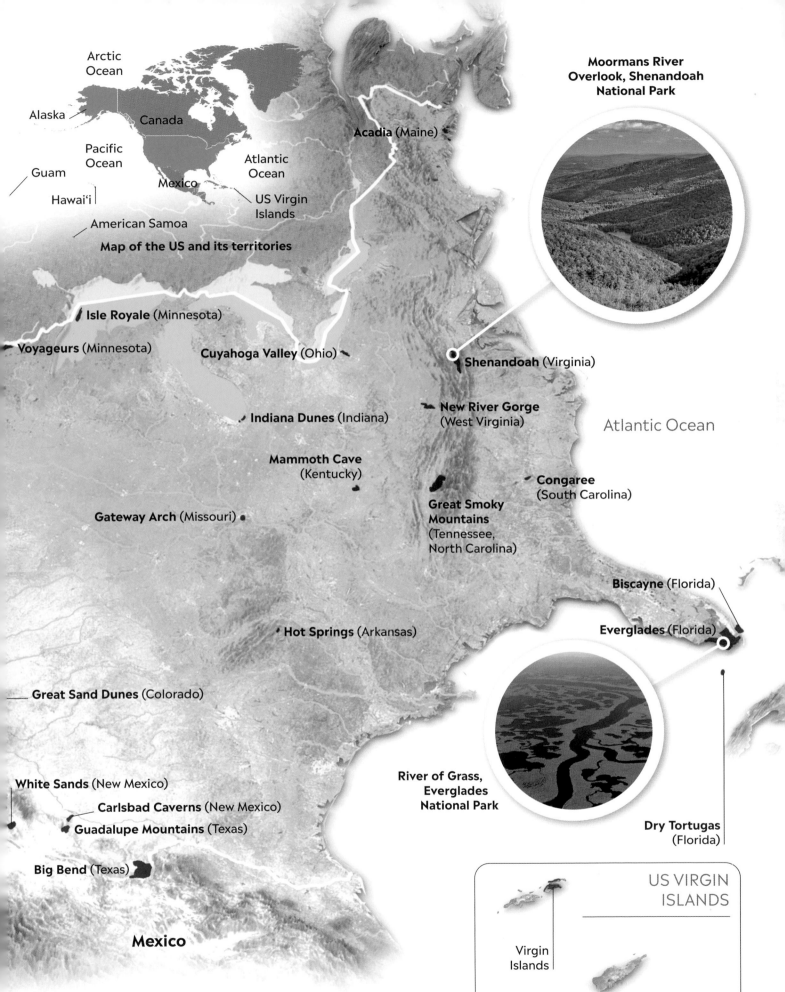

Arctic
Ocean

Alaska

Canada

Pacific
Ocean

Guam

Mexico

Hawai'i

Atlantic
Ocean

US Virgin
Islands

American Samoa

Map of the US and its territories

**Moormans River
Overlook, Shenandoah
National Park**

Acadia (Maine)

Isle Royale (Minnesota)

Voyageurs (Minnesota)

Cuyahoga Valley (Ohio)

Shenandoah (Virginia)

Atlantic Ocean

New River Gorge
(West Virginia)

Indiana Dunes (Indiana)

Mammoth Cave
(Kentucky)

Congaree
(South Carolina)

Gateway Arch (Missouri)

**Great Smoky
Mountains**
(Tennessee,
North Carolina)

Biscayne (Florida)

Everglades (Florida)

Hot Springs (Arkansas)

Great Sand Dunes (Colorado)

**River of Grass,
Everglades
National Park**

White Sands (New Mexico)

Carlsbad Caverns (New Mexico)

Guadalupe Mountains (Texas)

Dry Tortugas
(Florida)

Big Bend (Texas)

Mexico

US VIRGIN
ISLANDS

Virgin
Islands

7

Biscayne

FLORIDA

Sparkling in the Florida sunshine, Biscayne earns its title as the "southern jewel" of the US's national park system. With a chain of lush, green islands, crystal-clear lagoons and bays, colorful coral reefs, and dense mangrove forests, this spectacular setting in the northern part of the Florida Keys is the only national park that is 95 percent water.

Island butterfly

First spotted in the Florida forests by US scientist William Schaus in 1911, the Schaus's swallowtail butterfly is currently endangered and found only in Biscayne. Thanks to conservation measures, numbers are slowly rising.

Yellow markings stand out against the dark wings.

N ↑

The Florida Keys, which run a length of 221 miles (355 km) in the Gulf of Mexico, divide Biscayne Bay from the Atlantic Ocean.

Biscayne Channel

Brewster Reef

Star Reef

Boca Chita Key

Sands Key

Biscayne Bay

Dante Fascell Visitor Center

Spite Highway Trail

Elliott Key

Mangrove Key

Totten Key

ATLANTIC OCEAN

Old Rhodes Key

0 km — 8
0 miles — 8

Florida manatee Hermit crab
Spiny lobster Atlantic bottlenose dolphin

Florida Keys

During the last ice age, sea levels fell, revealing the fossilized coral reefs now known as the Florida Keys. This eye-catching strip of tropical islands avoids erosion and remains stable thanks to the tangled roots of mangrove forests.

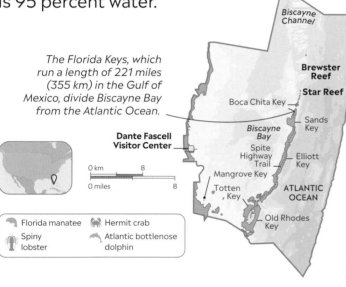

Underwater wrecks

In the past, stormy waters and hidden reefs made this area one of the world's most dangerous routes for ships. The Maritime Heritage Trail at Biscayne stands testament to this time with at least 40 shipwrecks on the ocean floor for snorkelers and scuba divers to explore.

Rainbow reefs

The warm waters of Biscayne Bay are home to a chain of coral reefs that teems with dolphins, sea turtles, and more than 200 types of fish, including parrotfish, goby, and queen angelfish. Divers can spend hours exploring this underwater world.

8

Out on the water

The best way to see the lagoons and bays of Biscayne is by boat. Locals and visitors use canoes, kayaks, and paddleboards to immerse themselves in the scenery and wildlife.

Oar-powered boats cause the least disturbance to marine life.

Hands-on learning

Park rangers at Biscayne run an educational program for students of all ages to experience marine science firsthand. There is a laboratory for water research and camping expeditions along the coastline.

A sifting box is used to separate sea shells from the surrounding sand.

👁 EYEWITNESS

Charles Lawson
Award-winning archaeologist Charles Lawson focuses on making archaeology more inclusive. His research on shipwrecks of ships that carried enslaved people aims to find out the lost history of many Black people in the US.

Everglades

FLORIDA

The Everglades National Park spans an enormous 1.5 million acres (610,000 ha) of land at Florida's southern tip. Its sprawling marshes and mangroves provide a welcome wetland for hundreds of different species of wildlife.

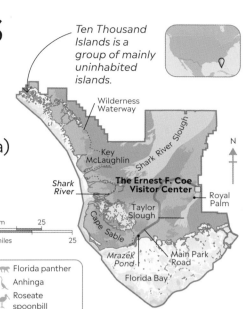

Ten Thousand Islands is a group of mainly uninhabited islands.

Wilderness Waterway

Shark River Slough

Key McLaughlin

Shark River

The Ernest F. Coe Visitor Center

Royal Palm

Taylor Slough

Cape Sable

Mrazek Pond

Main Park Road

Florida Bay

N

0 km — 25
0 miles — 25

- Florida panther
- Anhinga
- Roseate spoonbill

The American alligator can grow to a length of 15 ft (4.5 m).

Park predator

American alligators stalk the park's swamplands and trails. The Everglades is the only place where alligators and crocodiles share the same habitat.

Dry Tortugas

FLORIDA

Like a perfect picture postcard, Dry Tortugas is an archipelago of seven islands lying in the crystal-clear waters of the Gulf of Mexico. This remote location has created a bountiful habitat for tropical marine life and birds.

N

0 km — 6
0 miles — 6

Northkey Harbor

Garden Key

Loggerhead Key

Fort Jefferson

Windjammer wreck

Brick Wreck is one of nearly 300 shipwrecks in the region.

- Hermit crab
- Magnificent frigatebird
- Great barracuda
- Nurse shark

Famous fort

Constructed in the 19th century, Fort Jefferson served as a Union military base and prison during the Civil War. Today, it is the nation's third-biggest fort and can be reached only by boat or seaplane.

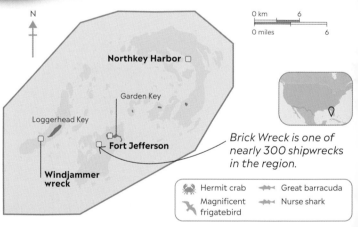

Airboat adventure

One of the best ways to explore the Everglades is by airboat. This fan-propelled boat glides over the shallow waters, while guides on board point out the incredible wildlife.

River of grass

Seen from the air, the wetlands of the Everglades resemble a gently flowing river of grass. This is why the Seminole people, who are indigenous to the region, named their home *Pahayokee*, which means "grassy waters."

The pink color comes from natural pigments in the birds' diet of shrimp and algae.

Fabulous flamingoes

Conservation programs have encouraged flamingoes to return to the Everglades National Park. These big-billed, long-necked wading birds are instantly recognizable for their striking pink color.

Turtle power

For centuries, turtles have been such a familiar sight on the islands that the national park was named Tortugas (Spanish for "turtles") after them. They nest on the islands and feed on mollusks and crabs in the waters of the park.

Loggerhead turtle

Deep dives

Scuba diving and snorkeling reveal this national park at its best. The underwater world is teeming with marine life—from giant sharks to tiny tropical fish—as well as many shipwrecks.

The six main walls of Fort Jefferson were built from more than 16 million bricks.

On the beach
Tourists flock to the beautiful beaches of the Virgin Islands, famed for their white sand, turquoise-colored waters, and snorkeling sites, such as Hawksnest Bay.

Virgin Islands
US VIRGIN ISLANDS

Sitting on the fringes of the Caribbean, this national park dominates the island of St. John. It offers plentiful tropical forests, white-sand beaches, and warm coral reefs, as well as ruins of many sugar plantations—a reminder of the region's history of slavery.

Hassel Island

Vessup Bay

North Shore Road

Honeymoon Beach

Johnson's Reef

Cinnamon Bay

Annaberg Sugar Plantation

Centerline Road

Cinnamon Bay Trail

☐ **Catherineberg Sugar Plantation**

Petroglyphs

🏛 **Visitor Center**

Reef Bay Sugar Mill

N

Reef Bay is one of the most popular beaches on the island of St. John.

0 km — 3
0 miles — 3

🐢 Hawksbill turtle 🦈 Whale shark
🐢 Green sea turtle 🦇 Greater
🐢 Leatherback turtle   bulldog bat

The flowers are typically white.

Night bloomer
The park's lush rainforests are home to more than 700 species of plants. One of them is the cereus cactus. Its flowers fill the night air with their sweet fragrance—they open shortly after dark before closing at sunrise. Some varieties bloom for only one night of the year.

Venomous visitor
The coral reefs and tropical waters provide a habitat for more than 300 species of fish. This spotted eagle ray, which can grow to a length of 16.4 ft (5 m), is best avoided, though, because its venomous tail spines are dangerous to divers.

Colorful fabric decorates the wooden stilts used by Moko Jumbies.

Dizzy heights
African influences remain part of the park's cultural history. The tradition of dancing by stilt walkers known as Moko Jumbies was introduced to the island by enslaved people brought here from West Africa by European colonizers.

Congaree

SOUTH CAROLINA

The US's largest expanse of low-lying hardwood forest is protected at Congaree National Park. Towering trees and dense foliage create a secluded space for wildlife to thrive.

Walk in the park

Stretching over a distance of 2 miles (4 km), this wooden boardwalk has been carefully constructed above treacherous areas of swampland. It allows visitors to wander safely through the wilderness.

Longleaf is one of the two designated campgrounds in the park.

Boardwalk

N

Wise Lake

Harry Hampton Visitor Center

Cedar Creek

Weston Lake Trail

Congaree River

Cedar Creek is a stream that flows through the center of Congaree.

0 km   4
0 miles   4

Barred owl	Question mark butterfly
River otter	Southern fox squirrel

Insects are the main part of this bird's diet.

Endangered woodpecker

Congaree is a haven for many birds, including hawks, owls, and woodpeckers. The red-cockaded woodpecker (right) is endangered in the US, but has found safety in the forests here.

Buttery blooms

Named after its buttery yellow flowers, the butterweed blooms in Congaree throughout spring. Its bright color attracts the attention of pollinators, such as bees and butterflies.

Cedar Creek

Canoeing or kayaking on the waters of Cedar Creek gives a breathtaking view of the tree species—from soaring cedars to sturdy oaks—growing in this floodplain forest. It also offers an opportunity to spot a variety of animals such as river otters, deer, and turtles.

Smoky view

This national park is named after the thick fog that often envelops its majestic mountains. This spectacular view of the sunrise over Clingmans Dome captures the cool blue hue of the morning fog.

Great Smoky Mountains

TENNESSEE, NORTH CAROLINA

With misty mountains, rushing waterfalls, and panoramic views, it is no wonder that the Great Smoky Mountains is the US's most visited national park. It is a sanctuary for more than 19,000 plant and animal species.

Cades Cove is a vast valley where members of the Cherokee Nation lived before 1819.

0 km 10
0 miles 10
N

Little River Road · Sugarlands Visitor Center · Ramsey Cascades · US Route 441 · Rainbow Falls · Appalachian Trail · Elkmont Campground · Observation Tower · Newfound Gap · Deep Creek · Cataloochee Creek · Cades Cove Paths · Clingmans Dome · Andrews Bald · Mingus Mill

TENNESSEE
NORTH CAROLINA

Eastern hognose snake | Brook trout
White-tailed deer | Striped skunk

Protected bears

The park is home to nearly 1,500 American black bears—that's up to two bears per square mile! These bears are mostly solitary, but protective mothers raise the cubs for almost two years.

👁 **EYEWITNESS**

Lavita Hill

For thousands of years, the Cherokee people called Clingmans Dome *Kuwohi*, meaning "mulberry place." Lavita Hill, who is a member of this nation, is one of the people working toward making Kuwohi the official name of this mountain.

14

Night lights

Nighttime in this national park is illuminated by fireflies flickering their lights to attract mates. Every June, crowds of visitors gather to see different types of fireflies as they synchronize their lights to turn on and off at the same time.

Salamander capital

Also known as the "salamander capital of the world," this park is a rich habitat for more than 30 species of salamanders, including this black-chinned red variety.

In 2021, more than
14 million people
visited this park.

Tubing hot spot

Water sports are discouraged in most places in this national park, except in Deep Creek near Bryson City. Here, adventure seekers can enjoy tubing downstream.

CONTROLLED BURN

Fires that are started under controlled conditions can remove dead wood and underbrush, as well as support some plants and animals. In the Smoky Mountain National Park, controlled fires help the table mountain pine's cones to open for dispersing seeds.

Firebreaks stop the fire from spreading beyond set borders.

The wind fans the flames in the direction it is blowing, making the fire burn faster.

Wind

Mammoth Cave

KENTUCKY

This national park contains a stunning underground system of caves that was discovered and mined by Indigenous people thousands of years ago. It is the world's longest known cave system, with 400 miles (640 km) already explored, as well as lush hills and river valleys.

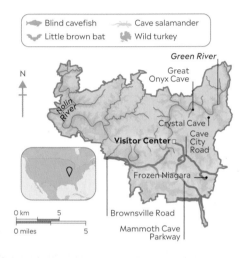

Key:
- Blind cavefish
- Little brown bat
- Cave salamander
- Wild turkey

N

Green River
Great Onyx Cave
Nolin River
Crystal Cave
Visitor Center
Cave City Road
Frozen Niagara
Brownsville Road
Mammoth Cave Parkway

0 km — 5
0 miles — 5

Cave creature
The Kentucky cave shrimp is found only in this national park. With no eyes and a tiny, transparent body, it moves through the caves feeling for food with its two antennae.

First guides
The first tours of Mammoth Cave were given by enslaved Black people in 1838. Among today's tour guides is Jerry Bransford, great-great-grandson of Mat Bransford (man on the left), who was one of the original tour guides.

CAVE CREATIONS

Mineral-filled water creates amazing structures inside caves. Dripping water collects on the ceiling to form hanging stalactites, while puddles of water on the ground make standing stalagmites. Over time, they may meet and form a pillar from floor to ceiling.

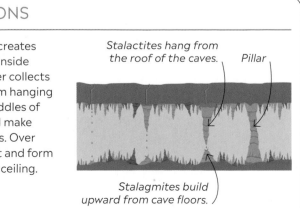

Stalactites hang from the roof of the caves.

Pillar

Stalagmites build upward from cave floors.

Underground wonder
Frozen Niagara is one of the most spectacular sections of Mammoth Cave. Visitors can go on a short walk to see these crystallized formations that resemble a frozen Niagara Falls in winter.

Shenandoah

VIRGINIA

A world away from the concrete jungle of nearby Washington, DC, is this wonderland of waterfalls, woodlands, and wildflowers in the Blue Ridge mountains.

Skyline Drive stretches 105 miles (168 km) and is the only road through the park.

Dickey Ridge Visitor Center

Big Meadows

Old Rag Mountain

Appalachian National Scenic Trail

N

0 km 10
0 miles 10

Shenandoah salamander
Hummingbird clearwing moth
Daddy long-legs spider
Scarlet tanager

Appalachian adventure

Shenandoah is located in the Blue Ridge section of the Appalachian Mountains. More than 100 miles (160 km) of a famous hiking trail called the Appalachian Trail, which is known for its scenic wilderness, lies inside the park.

Morel mushrooms

There are more than 400 species of fungi in Shenandoah. Morel mushrooms (right) are easy to spot, but there are many poisonous mushrooms in the park, so it is best not to pick any without guidance.

New River Gorge

WEST VIRGINIA

Despite its name, this park's New River is actually the oldest river in the US. Whitewater kayakers enjoy the rapids, while the surrounding forested mountains are a haven for hikers.

Coyote
North American raccoon
White-tailed deer
Green sunfish

0 km 10
0 miles 10

New River Gorge Bridge

Canyon Rim Visitor Center

N

New River

Route 64

Sandstone Falls

Bridging the gap

The New River Gorge Bridge took three years to build in the 1970s and was then the world's longest steel arch bridge. An annual festival celebrating this engineering marvel is known as "Bridge Day."

Peregrine program

Experts raise peregrine falcon chicks at New River Gorge with minimal human contact before releasing them when they are old enough to fly. This program aims to increase the region's declining number of falcons.

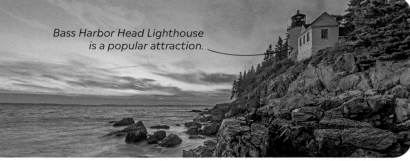
Bass Harbor Head Lighthouse is a popular attraction.

Mount Desert Island

The largest island off the coast of Maine is Mount Desert Island. It was named by French colonist Samuel de Champlain, who visited in 1604. Today, this picturesque island is part of the park and home to 10,000 people.

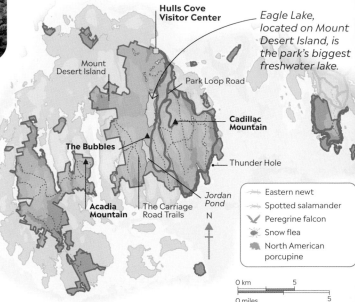

Hulls Cove Visitor Center

Eagle Lake, located on Mount Desert Island, is the park's biggest freshwater lake.

Mount Desert Island

Park Loop Road

Cadillac Mountain

The Bubbles

Thunder Hole

Jordan Pond

Acadia Mountain

The Carriage Road Trails

N

- Eastern newt
- Spotted salamander
- Peregrine falcon
- Snow flea
- North American porcupine

0 km   5
0 miles   5

Acadia

MAINE

One of the most visited national parks, Acadia lies off the coast of Maine with granite mountains, rugged headlands, and idyllic lakes. The changing seasons reveal the vivid colors of the forest in fall and a pristine blanket of snow in winter.

Lake loons

Every year, common loons arrive in Acadia to use the park's plentiful lakes as feeding and nesting grounds. They are easy to spot with black heads, red eyes, and noisy calls.

Shiny, striped neck

Thunder wonder

A feature of Acadia's coastline is Thunder Hole, a rocky inlet that has formed naturally from water erosion. As the tide rushes in and hits the rocks, the waves are forced as high as 40 ft (12 m), producing a loud clapping sound like thunder and splashing on visitors on the park's coastal walkways.

 EYEWITNESS

Bonnie Newsom

Dr. Bonnie Newsom is a citizen of the Penobscot Nation. An experienced archaeologist, she is one of the people studying Acadia's archaeological collections to highlight the Wabanaki ("People of the Dawnland"), an Indigenous people who have lived here for 12,000 years.

Top view of Thunder Hole

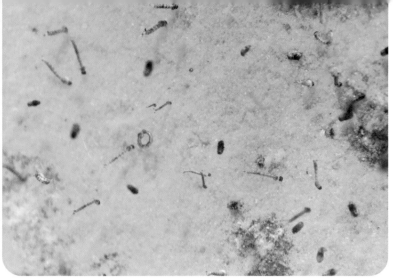

Algal blooms

Harmful algae blooms are appearing in Acadia's lakes, as a result of global warming and environmental damage. Blooms become out of control, polluting the water. Scientists are creating warning systems that detect new blooms to protect the lakes.

The constant crashing of the waves erodes the granite ridges on the coast.

Acadia is named after
Arcadia
in Greece that shares a similar landscape.

Fluffy body with yellow and pink wings

Many moths

At least 180 types of moths live in Acadia. Moths are essential for the ecosystem, providing an important food source for bats, birds, and some large insects. Most moths are dark and dull, but varieties such as this rosy maple moth are bright.

Canal Exploration Center

North American beaver
Muskrat
American mink
Painted turtle

Ohio & Erie Canalway America's Byway
Ohio & Erie Canal Towpath Trail
Cuyahoga Scenic Railroad
Brandywine Falls
Boston Mill Visitor Center
Cuyahoga River
Beaver Marsh

N

0 km   4
0 miles   4

Cuyahoga Valley

OHIO

The Cuyahoga ("crooked river" in the Iroquoian group of languages) winds through nearly 33,000 acres (13,300 ha) of leafy woodlands, deep valleys, and open fields in this national park. Visitors can try hiking, kayaking, and even skiing.

Wildlife watching

Much of the park wildlife congregates at Beaver Marsh, including birds, turtles, frogs, and beavers working on the wetlands. A raised boardwalk provides a great spot to watch wildlife.

Frequent fliers

Cuyahoga Valley provides a pit stop for monarch butterflies during their epic migration of 3,000 miles (4,800 km) from Canada to Mexico. In summer, they lay their eggs on milkweed—the only plant that their young can eat after they hatch.

Indiana Dunes

INDIANA

Among the most biodiverse parks in the US, Indiana Dunes is a winning combination of beaches, forests, dunes, lakes, marshes, and more—with 50 miles (80 km) of hiking trails to enjoy the landscape.

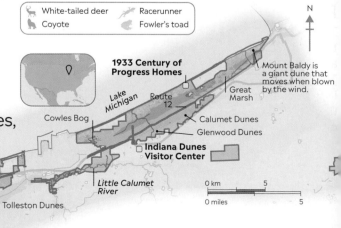

White-tailed deer
Coyote
Racerunner
Fowler's toad

N

1933 Century of Progress Homes
Mount Baldy is a giant dune that moves when blown by the wind.
Lake Michigan
Route 12
Great Marsh
Cowles Bog
Calumet Dunes
Glenwood Dunes
Indiana Dunes Visitor Center
Little Calumet River
Tolleston Dunes

0 km   5
0 miles   5

Cuyahoga Valley Scenic Railroad

Trains have run through the park for over a century. Today, the Cuyahoga Valley Scenic Railroad gives visitors a spectacular, steam-powered tour with running commentary from park rangers.

River restoration

The Cuyahoga River was plagued by human pollution in the past. Removing a major dam has improved oxygen levels and enhanced the natural flow of the water to help fish populations.

Sands of time

The biggest collection of freshwater dunes lies on the shores of Lake Michigan. They formed more than 13,000 years ago when westerly winds deposited large volumes of sand. A plant called beach grass thrives in the sandy soil. Its long blades slow the wind and catch windblown sand, helping the dunes grow.

Predatory plant

The park's wetlands are home to wading birds, flying insects, and even carnivorous plants. This pitcher plant traps insects and eats them slowly, using special digestive glands on the inside of its leaves.

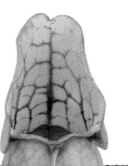

Budding photographers can capture the park's diverse views.

Spoiled for choice

A network of trails offers visitors the choice between beautiful beaches against a backdrop of dramatic dunes or wetland marshes and bogs, which attract an incredible range of wildlife.

21

Island plants

More than 400 islands make up Isle Royale. The islands are covered with conifer and deciduous trees, more than 600 species of flowering plants, and aquatic grasses, which are eaten by moose.

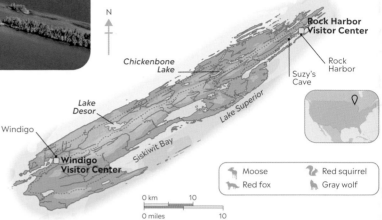

N

Rock Harbor Visitor Center

Rock Harbor

Chickenbone Lake

Suzy's Cave

Lake Desor

Lake Superior

Windigo

Windigo Visitor Center

Siskiwit Bay

Moose   Red squirrel
Red fox   Gray wolf

0 km   10
0 miles   10

Isle Royale

MICHIGAN

This national park sits on one main island and hundreds of smaller islands and islets in the middle of Lake Superior—one of the world's largest lakes. Nearly 99 percent of the park is wilderness.

Park pits

Indigenous people first began mining copper on Isle Royale about 4,500 years ago. The remains of hundreds of mining pits have been discovered on the island, together with ancient handcrafted copper tools.

Predator and prey

The gray wolf is Isle Royale's top predator, preying on moose—a relationship that has been studied on the island for over 40 years. The numbers of wolves and moose change year by year—when one goes up, the other goes down. When the wolf population declined to very low levels in 2011 and 2014, the authorities began introducing wolves to the park.

Backpacker's paradise

Isle Royale offers backpackers epic hikes with spectacular scenery, coastal views, and lush forest. There are at least 36 different campsites accessible either by boat or on foot. Hikers can take about 4–6 days to cover the 45-mile (72-km) length of the island between Windigo and Rock Harbor.

Voyageurs
MINNESOTA

Covering a huge expanse close to the Canadian border, Voyageurs is a combination of vast waterways, rugged islands, and thick forests. The waterways were once used as travel routes by French-Canadian voyageurs—fur traders from Canada who exchanged goods for beaver fur from the local Ojibwe people.

Adventures on ice
Plummeting winter temperatures cause lakes to freeze, creating a playground for winter sports. Once the National Park Service confirms the ice is suitably thick and safe, two ice roads are opened. Visitors can then choose between driving, skiing, or snowshoe hiking.

A day on the water
About one-third of Voyageurs is covered by water, making swimming, canoeing, kayaking, and fishing popular ways to experience the park. Campsites are located along the shoreline.

Rainy Lake Visitor Center

0 km 7
0 miles 7

Rainy Lake is a freshwater lake crossing Minnesota into Canada.

N

Ellsworth Rock Gardens

Cruiser Lake Trail

Namakan Lake

Echo Bay Trail

Kabetogama Lake Visitor Center

Ash River Visitor Center

Grassy Bay Cliffs

Sand Point Lake

Black bear
Common raven
Common loon
Bobcat
Canada lynx
North American beaver

The flower is named after its resemblance to a slipper.

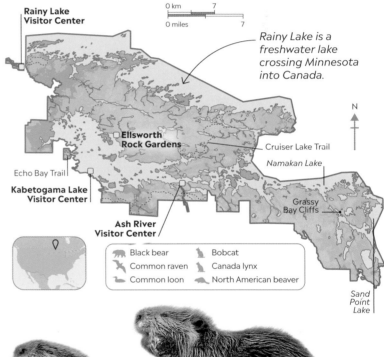

Lady's slipper
The state flower of Minnesota is the lady's slipper. This hardy, eye-catching orchid blooms in this national park during the summer months. It can be spotted easily near the Kabetogama Lake Visitor Center.

Builder beavers
Thousands of American beavers take advantage of the plentiful water and forest at Voyageurs. They dam up the rivers and streams to make private ponds where they build strong lodges out of wood and mud to raise their young.

Sizzling springs
Scorching hot, mineral-rich water emerges from the ground through 47 thermal springs. In 1832, a law was passed to protect the land and water in this area.

Hot Springs
ARKANSAS

One of the smallest national parks, Hot Springs covers an area of only 9 sq miles (23 sq km). Its historical bathhouses were fed with the nearby mineral-laden waters.

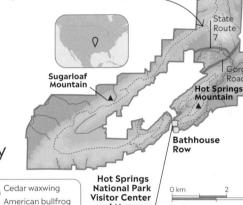

Sunset Trail makes for the longest hike in Hot Springs.

N

State Route 7

Sugarloaf Mountain ▲

Gorge Road

Hot Springs Mountain ▲

Bathhouse Row

Hot Springs National Park Visitor Center and Museum

| White-tailed deer | Cedar waxwing |
| Tricolored bat | American bullfrog |

0 km   2
0 miles   2

From the past
People have found many objects dating as far back as 8000 BCE in this park. Indigenous people living here would quarry novaculite, or Arkansas Stone, to make different tools and weapons such as the one above.

City landmark
Completed in 1965, this eye-catching stainless steel structure stands 630 ft (192 m) tall. It is the tallest monument in the US and the tallest arch in the world.

Gateway Arch
MISSOURI

Taking center stage at this national park is the star sight of St. Louis—the impressive Gateway Arch, which is surrounded by parkland on the banks of the Mississippi River. It was built to memorialize the purchase of the state of Louisiana by the US in 1803.

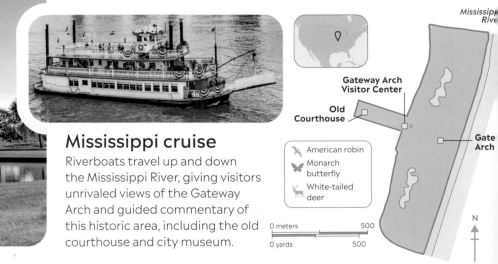

Mississippi cruise
Riverboats travel up and down the Mississippi River, giving visitors unrivaled views of the Gateway Arch and guided commentary of this historic area, including the old courthouse and city museum.

Mississippi River

Gateway Arch Visitor Center

Old Courthouse

Gateway Arch

| American robin |
| Monarch butterfly |
| White-tailed deer |

0 meters   500
0 yards   500

N

Wind Cave

SOUTH DAKOTA

At ground level, Wind Cave National Park has vast prairies and dense forests, which provide a home for wildlife. Below ground lies one of the longest and oldest caves in the world. This was the first cave system ever to be protected as a national park.

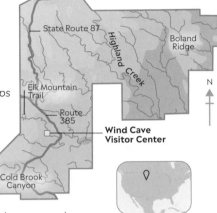

American bison

The population of the American bison in this region plummeted in the 19th century because of hunting. Thanks to the protection provided by this national park, hundreds of bison roam here today.

Boxwork is a rare honeycomb-shaped structure created when calcite fills gaps in limestone.

Boxwork

0 km 3
0 miles 3

State Route 87
Highland Creek
Boland Ridge
Elk Mountain Trail
Route 385
Wind Cave Visitor Center
Cold Brook Canyon

N

- Black-footed ferret
- Mountain lion
- Coyote
- Mule deer

Windy wonder

Named after the strong winds that blow around the entrance, Wind Cave has 150 miles (240 km) of underground tunnels. It also contains boxwork crystalline rock formations.

Badlands

SOUTH DAKOTA

The Indigenous Lakota people named this area Mako Sica ("land bad") for its treacherous terrain, unpredictable weather, and water shortage. But the national park also offers colorful canyons, peaceful prairies, and fascinating fossils.

Coloring the past

The striped layers of sedimentary rock correspond with different points of time in the region's geological past. The oldest rock layer is at the bottom, while the youngest rocks sit at the top.

Roberts Prairie Dog Town
Sage Creek
Badlands Loop Road
NORTH UNIT
Badland Wall
Ben Reifel Visitor Center
STRONGHOLD UNIT
PALMER CREEK UNIT

N

0 km 15
0 miles 15

Fossil finds

The park is rich in fossils of different mammals, including camels, horses, and rodents. The laboratory where scientists study these fossils is open to the public.

- American bison
- Pronghorn
- Golden eagle
- Prairie dog

Ancient swamp

On display in the visitor center, this Fossil Lake Wannagan mural shows an artist's interpretation of the area 65 million years ago when it was swampland. Today, the landscape is transformed with forests, floodplains, and badlands.

Theodore Roosevelt

NORTH DAKOTA

	Pronghorn
	American badger
	American bison
	Garter snake

0 km · · · · · · 15
0 miles · · · · · · 15

Named after the former US president, Theodore Roosevelt National Park stands testament to his lifelong commitment to conservation. The Little Missouri River weaves its way through the Badlands rock formations in this scenic expanse.

NORTH UNIT
Scenic Drive
Little Missouri River
ELKHORN RANCH
Scenic Loop Drive
N
Painted Canyon Visitor Center
SOUTH UNIT

Brilliant Badlands

The striped rocks of the Badlands took millions of years to form. These sedimentary rock deposits were shaped by sun, wind, and rain, and carved by the flow of the Little Missouri River. Natural erosion exposed their multicolored layers.

Big Bend

TEXAS

	Swallowtail butterfly		Mountain lion
	Big Bend scorpion		Green kingfisher

A "gift to the nation" from Texas, Big Bend is celebrated for its incredible range of wildlife and star-studded nights in the Chihuahuan Desert. The park's diverse history comes to life in the form of fossils, abandoned mines, and Indigenous artifacts.

N
Panther Junction Visitor Center
Ross Maxwell Scenic Drive
Chihuahuan Desert
Chisos Mountains
Santa Elena Canyon
Rio Grande River

A bend in the river

The Rio Grande River flows along the southern border for 118 miles (190 km). The park was named after the "big bend" in the river, where the water flow changes from southeast to northeast.

0 km · · · · · 20
0 miles · · · · · 20

Wild horses

This is the only national park in the US where wild horses roam free. There are over 150 horses at any given time, found only in the South Unit of the park. Visitors are advised to not approach these wild animals.

Layers of sand, silt, and mud were turned to stone over millions of years.

Superbloom

The bluebonnet is the official state flower of Texas. Most years, they grow in pretty patches alongside other wildflowers. However, heavy rainfall can create "superblooms" that cover entire hillsides in an eye-catching carpet of blue.

Colossal crocs

This life-sized bronze replica of a crocodile's jaws in the park's Fossil Discovery Exhibit pays homage to the predator that lived alongside dinosaurs. Fossils discovered at the Aguja Formation at Big Bend reveal giant crocodiles measuring 50 ft (15 m) long!

Off-road adventures

This remote location has many dirt roads suited to four-wheel driving. Big Bend is also the only national park with a gas station to fill up!

Carlsbad Caverns

NEW MEXICO

Beneath the Chihuahuan Desert lies a spectacular underground network of more than 100 limestone caves. Formed between 4 and 6 million years ago, Carlsbad Caverns is one of the best preserved cave systems on Earth.

Bat colony

An enormous colony of Brazilian free-tailed bats roosts inside the caves during summer, when up to a million bats fly from the caves every evening, creating an amazing aerial spectacle for visitors.

Inside the cave

The caves are easily accessible via the natural entrance for hikers or an elevator from the visitor center. Day trippers can explore vast chambers, including dramatic rock formations. Park rangers are also available for guided tours.

N

Visitor Center

Rattlesnake Canyon Trail

0 km   12

0 miles   12

Slaughter Canyon Cave can be seen only on a ranger-guided tour.

Yucca Canyon Trail

- Cave cricket
- Long-tailed weasel
- Gray fox
- Bobcat
- Black bear

White Sands

NEW MEXICO

This dazzling white landscape is the world's largest gypsum dunefield. Its sweeping mounds of gypsum sand create a truly unique desert, which is popular with hikers and sand sledders alike.

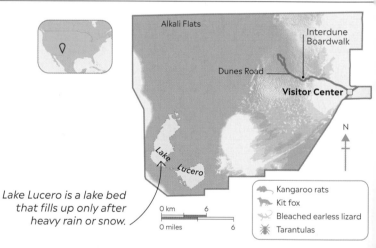

Alkali Flats

Interdune Boardwalk

Dunes Road

Visitor Center

N

Lake Lucero

Lake Lucero is a lake bed that fills up only after heavy rain or snow.

0 km   6

0 miles   6

- Kangaroo rats
- Kit fox
- Bleached earless lizard
- Tarantulas

Gypsum dunefield

Covering 275 sq miles (710 sq km), this record-breaking dunefield is created by crystals of a mineral called gypsum that form in Lake Lucero as the water evaporates. The crystals break up over time and blow in the wind, forming the dunes.

Guadalupe Mountains

TEXAS

Deserts, mountains, and canyons meet in Guadalupe Mountains National Park. This area protects a rugged mountain ecosystem and the greatest Permian fossil reef on Earth. Humans have lived here for over 10,000 years.

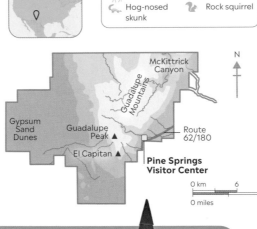

Mule deer
Hog-nosed skunk
Ringtail
Rock squirrel

McKittrick Canyon
Guadalupe Mountains
Gypsum Sand Dunes
Guadalupe Peak ▲
El Capitan ▲
Route 62/180
Pine Springs Visitor Center
N
0 km 6
0 miles 6

Reaching the peak

At 8,750 ft (2,667 m) above sea level, Guadalupe Peak is the highest point in the Guadalupe Mountain Range and the tallest point in Texas. The challenging hike rewards visitors with unparalleled views of the landscape, including desert dunes.

Forest in fall

The McKittrick Canyon Trail is a well-traveled path surrounded by hardwood forest. Here, visitors flock to enjoy the changing colors of the fall foliage, against the scenic, steep-sided canyon backdrop.

Fossilized footprints

White Sands is home to the oldest human footprints ever found in North America. Researchers discovered footprints fossilized in gypsum soil and used radiocarbon dating to estimate they are 23,000 years old.

Ancient human footprints

Sledding down a dune

Great Sand Dunes
COLORADO

Sandboarding, camping, and offroading are all great ways of enjoying this national park. The tallest sand dunes in North America lie at its heart, but walking trails lead to other habitats, including forests and lakes. This park ranks among the US's quietest national parks.

Ancient cultures

People have lived in what is now the park area for 11,000 years. The region is sacred to many Indigenous peoples, including the Apache, Dine, Pueblo, and Ute. Visitors can learn about their ancient traditions by attending national park talks by Indigenous people from the area.

Desert hunter

Native to Colorado, the Great Sand Dunes tiger beetle is a fast-moving hunter that scurries across the sand looking for tasty insects.

Kangaroo rat
Mule deer
Mountain lion
Abert's squirrel

Map: Sangre de Cristo Mountains, Star Dune Complex, Dunefield, Medano Creek, Visitor Center, State Highway 150

0 km 8
0 miles 8

Sand stars

The park's dramatic dunes reach about 700 ft (210 m) in height. The tallest one—called Star Dune—towers over its surroundings at 750 ft (229 m).

Still waters

Rocky Mountain has at least 150 alpine lakes, reflecting the majestic mountains around them. They formed when glaciers forged canyons and hollows where pools of water collected. Most lakes are accessible by marked trails.

Rocky Mountain
COLORADO

This national park is an alpine dream of snowcapped peaks, pristine lakes, and evergreen forests. With more than 300 miles (480 km) of hiking trails, Rocky Mountain is known for high elevations, panoramic views, thriving wildlife, and camping opportunities.

Map: Alpine Visitor Center, Trail Ridge Road, Continental Divide, Beaver Meadows Entrance, Estes Park, Grand Lake

Black bear
Yellow-bellied marmot
North American porcupine
North American elk
Gray jay
Mountain chickadee

0 km 10
0 miles 10

The pika

American pikas are small, squeaking mammals found in mountainous environments. Pikas thrive in this national park—they can be seen darting around rocky areas near walking trails.

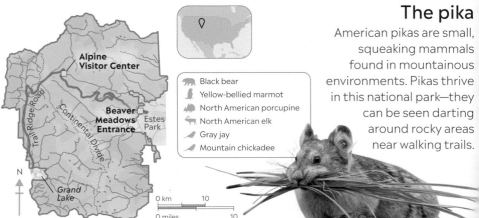

River deep

The Gunnison River and natural erosion have together carved this colossal, craggy canyon over two million years. It is so deep that sunlight hardly ever reaches the bottom, giving it the name Black Canyon.

Aerial hunter

Great horned owls frequent the park because rabbits and rodents run around even in winter. Named after their tufty ears, these giant birds use lofty canyon rims to spot prey from above.

Black Canyon of the Gunnison

COLORADO

The deep canyons, steep-sided cliffs, and soaring spires of this national park offer many natural wonders, including the Gunnison River rapids and the Painted Wall—Colorado's tallest cliff. The Ute people referred to the area as "much rocks, big water."

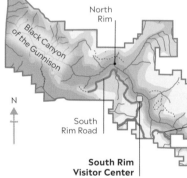

North Rim

Black Canyon of the Gunnison

N

South Rim Road

South Rim Visitor Center

East Portal Road

Mountain cottontail	Bobcat
Long-tailed weasel	Rocky Mountain bighorn sheep
Golden eagle	

0 — 5 km
0 — 5 miles

Snow season

Winter snowfall closes the South Rim Drive to vehicles. At this time, seasonal activities change to cross-country skiing and snowshoeing on the rim. Activities in the canyon are discouraged.

Yellowstone

WYOMING, MONTANA, IDAHO

In 1872, Yellowstone became the US's first national park, named after the Yellowstone River that weaves its way through it. Bubbling mud pots, gushing geysers, and colorful hot springs dot this natural spa, which is home to a wide range of large animals.

The Grand Prismatic Spring is the US's largest and the **world's third-largest** hot spring.

Wolf revival

Gray wolves were hunted to near extinction in the park a century ago until scientists recognized their importance in the food chain. They were reintroduced in small numbers in 1995, and the population is now thriving.

Old Faithful

Known for its regular eruptions, Old Faithful geyser delights millions of visitors each year. It still erupts every 90 minutes a day—more often than most giant geysers. Each eruption can last up to 5 minutes and reach a height of 106–180 ft (30–55 m).

👁 EYEWITNESS

Douglas Smith
Wildlife expert Douglas Smith has studied wolves for more than 40 years. He leads the Wolf Restoration Project at Yellowstone—his work has helped to reintroduce gray wolves as park predators to create a natural, balanced ecosystem and protect this endangered species.

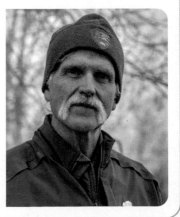

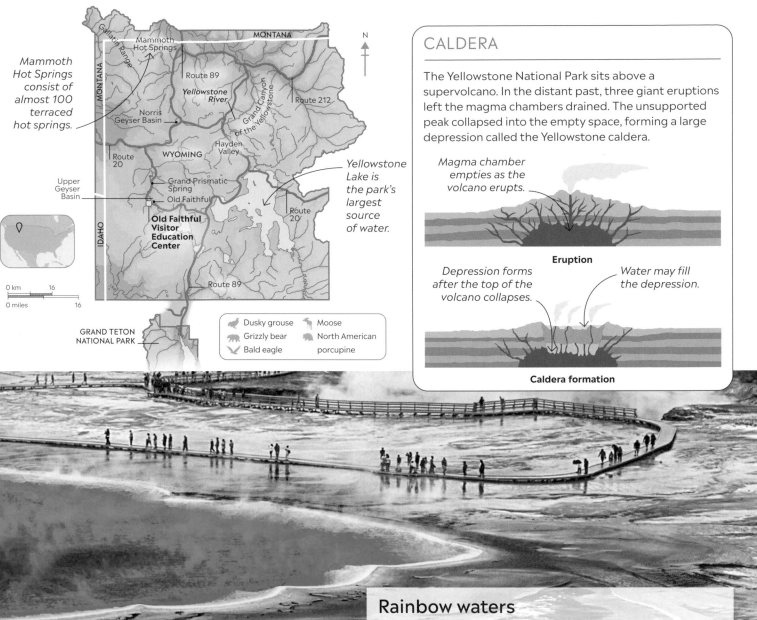

Mammoth Hot Springs consist of almost 100 terraced hot springs.

Mammoth Hot Springs

Gallatin Range

MONTANA

MONTANA

Route 89

Yellowstone River

Route 212

Norris Geyser Basin

Grand Canyon of the Yellowstone

Route 20

WYOMING

Hayden Valley

Upper Geyser Basin

Grand Prismatic Spring

Old Faithful

Old Faithful Visitor Education Center

Yellowstone Lake is the park's largest source of water.

Route 20

IDAHO

N

0 km   16
0 miles   16

Route 89

GRAND TETON NATIONAL PARK

	Dusky grouse		Moose
	Grizzly bear		North American porcupine
	Bald eagle		

CALDERA

The Yellowstone National Park sits above a supervolcano. In the distant past, three giant eruptions left the magma chambers drained. The unsupported peak collapsed into the empty space, forming a large depression called the Yellowstone caldera.

Magma chamber empties as the volcano erupts.

Eruption

Depression forms after the top of the volcano collapses.

Water may fill the depression.

Caldera formation

Rainbow waters

The kaleidoscopic colors of the Grand Prismatic Spring make it look like a painter's palette. The colors come from pigments in bacteria and algae that flourish in the sizzling hot, mineral-rich waters.

Winter adventure

During the winter season, Yellowstone is usually transformed by heavy snowfall and subzero temperatures. Snowmobiles are available for rent and visitors can book guided tours to explore the park.

Bring on the bison

This park is the only place in the US where bison have lived continuously since prehistoric times. Herds regularly cause bison jams when thousands cross the roads at once! Male bison may be seen fighting during mating season.

Teton Peaks

Part of the Rocky Mountains, the Teton Range, which spans 40 miles (64 km), is one of the youngest mountain ranges in the world. The Snake River runs at the base of the mountains and is visited by all kinds of wildlife, including moose.

Grand Teton

WYOMING

Named after its location at the heart of the Teton mountain range, Grand Teton is an impressive combination of snowy peaks, alpine lakes, and lush lowlands. Visitors have many activities to choose from, including wildlife watching, water sports, hiking, driving scenic roadways, and visiting nearly 700 historical sites!

YELLOWSTONE NATIONAL PARK

Jackson Lake sits at more than 6,500 ft (2,000 m) above sea level.

John D. Rockefeller, Jr Memorial Parkway

Teton Range

Teton Park Road

Oxbow Bend

Jenny Lake

Jackson Hole

Snake River

N

Mormon Row

Craig Thomas Discovery and Visitor Center

0 km   12
0 miles   12

- 🐻 Grizzly bear
- 🐻 Black bear
- Yellow-bellied marmot
- 🫎 Moose
- 🦌 Elk
- Trumpeter swan

Paddleboarding park

While there are several lakes and rivers for standup paddleboarding (SUP) at Grand Teton, String Lake is ideal for beginners. It has a soft, sandy bed and calm waters. Jenny Lake is the most popular spot for this activity, but it gets stronger winds.

Winged wonder

Weighing the same as a ping pong ball, the calliope hummingbird is the smallest bird in the US. It is named after Calliope, the Greek muse of heroic poetry. It nests in the national park, alongside osprey, swans, and eagles.

Males have shiny, magenta neck feathers.

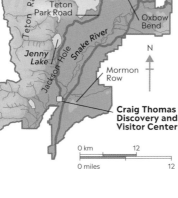

Wild flowers

Native to the US, the common camas is just one of many beautiful wildflowers that bloom throughout the park every summer. Wildflowers provide food and habitat for animals and birds.

Youth corps

Since 2016, a group of young Indigenous people have championed preservation projects at Grand Teton as part of the Tribal Youth Corps. The program aims to support career opportunities in conservation at the national park.

Icy climb
Treacherous ice climbing up steep slopes in Glacier National Park is not for the fainthearted. Ice axes and spiked boots are essential to get a grip on the slippery surface.

Glacier
MONTANA

Living up to its name, Glacier National Park stands testament to millennia of glacier activity. Deep valleys, alpine mountains, and more than 700 miles (1,125 km) of trails draw hikers, cyclists, and campers to this welcoming wilderness.

Iceberg Lake
Many Glacier ▲
St. Mary Visitor Center
Grinnell Glacier ▲
Logan Pass ▲
N
Lake McDonald
Going-to-the-Sun Road
Two Medicine Lake
0 km   20
0 miles   20

Canada lynx   Wolverines
Mountain goat   White-tailed ptarmigan

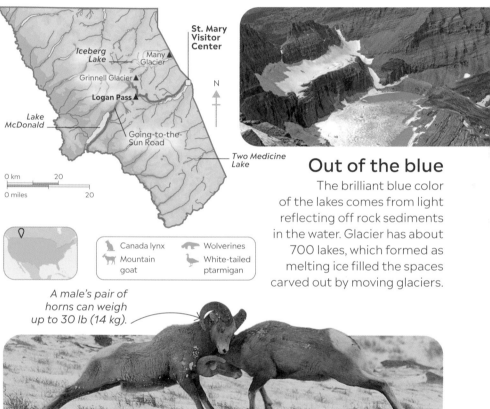

Out of the blue
The brilliant blue color of the lakes comes from light reflecting off rock sediments in the water. Glacier has about 700 lakes, which formed as melting ice filled the spaces carved out by moving glaciers.

A male's pair of horns can weigh up to 30 lb (14 kg).

Bighorn battle
A large herd of bighorn sheep inhabits Glacier National Park. These agile mountaineers fight using their horns as weapons. The deafening sound of clashing horns can be heard 1 mile (1.6 km) away.

GLACIERS

Glaciers are the largest source of fresh water on Earth. They form when snow builds up, compresses into a thick block of ice, and slowly moves downward to the sea. Because of climate change, Glacier National Park has lost more than 67 percent of its glaciers since 1850!

Fallen snow piles up and turns to ice over time.

A stream or lake can form as the glacier melts.

The glacier flows slowly downhill.

Mesa Verde
COLORADO

Rocky Mountain elk
American badger
Mexican spotted owl

0 km 6
0 miles 6

N

Mesa Verde National
Park Visitor and
Research Center

Wetherill
Mesa Road

Mesa Top
Ruins Road

Long
House

Cliff Palace
is the largest
cliff dwelling
in the US.

Balcony House

Since it opened in 1906, Mesa Verde has protected a collection of 5,000 archaeological sites, including 600 cliff dwellings. It is the first US national park to preserve the "works" of people rather than nature.

Puebloan past

Ancestral Pueblo people lived in this region for more than 700 years. They constructed hundreds of homes among the cliffs and canyons, as well as ceremonial centers, called kivas.

Larvae lunch

The beautiful black swallowtail butterfly is a common sight in Mesa Verde. Its young larvae feast on the rare Mesa Verde wandering aletes, a plant found in the park.

Capitol Reef
UTAH

The rocky layers of this park, which resemble an ocean reef, include canyons, cliffs, and domes—all shaped by Waterpocket Fold, a vast surface crumple caused by erosion.

Cathedral Valley

Capitol Reef Visitor Center

Capitol Dome

State Route 24

Golden Throne

Scenic Drive

Waterpocket Fold

N

Ringtail
Utah prairie dog
Canyon tree frog

0 km 22
0 miles 22

Mountain king

Mountain lions lie low in the rocky hideaways of Capitol Reef. They hunt at dawn and dusk by stalking deer, coyote, and rabbits. Their hunting keeps prey numbers down and prevents the park from becoming overpopulated.

Mail tree

Capitol Reef's most visited tree is this Fremont cottonwood. During the 19th century, this was the mail tree where locals hung their post on the branches ready for collection.

Canyonlands

UTAH

The largest national park in Utah is a desert landscape carved by the natural flow of the Colorado and Green rivers. Visitors are spoiled for choice with hiking, climbing, camping, and stargazing.

Island in the Sky Visitor Center
Horseshoe Canyon
Grand View Point Road
N
Island in the Sky
Green River
Colorado River
The Maze
State Route 211
The Needles

0 km 14
0 miles 14

🦋 Yucca moth
🐏 Bighorn sheep
🦅 Canyon wren
🐦 Common Raven

On the rocks

Most of the plentiful rocks at Canyonlands cannot be climbed because they are too weak or impossible to access. The steep sandstone cliffs of Island in the Sky offer safe climbing with panoramic views.

Sharp as needles

The Needles take center stage in a remote part of the park. These red-rock pillars of sandstone stand tall and pointed and extend for many miles.

People have lived in Canyonlands for at least 10,000 years.

Arches

UTAH

0 km 7
0 miles 7

🦉 Burrowing owl
🐀 Kangaroo rat
🐸 Great Basin spadefoot toad

Devil's Garden
Landscape Arch
Fiery Furnace
Delicate Arch
Double Arch
Arches National Park Road
N
Arches Visitor Center

Devil's Garden is a collection of arches in different shapes and sizes.

Awesome arch

Measuring 46 ft (14 m) tall, Delicate Arch is the largest free-standing arch in the park and a famous Utah landmark. It is only accessible after a steep climb, but this grand view is a welcome reward.

Living up to its name, this park plays host to more than 2,000 sandstone arches in the Utah desert. But this is just one example of many different rock formations at Arches, including pinnacles, columns, towers, and spires.

Super soil

Plants in the park rely on microorganisms, including bacteria, algae, and fungi, for survival. These microorganisms form layers in the sandy soil, called biological soil crusts, that produce essential nutrients and trap moisture for plants to grow. Visitors are advised not to step on these crusts!

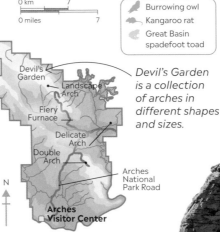

Zion

UTAH

Known for its rich canyons carved by the Virgin River, steep cliffs, and dramatic viewpoints, Utah's first national park has something for everyone. Adventurous explorers can reach dizzy heights with a strenuous climb up to Angels Landing, while families may prefer an easy hike to the waterfalls along the Emerald Pools Trail.

Taking the Subway

The Subway is a red-rock canyon named after its similar shape to the New York City Subway. This park landmark is perfect for visitors who love canyoneering—a combination of different activities, including hiking, rappelling, and route finding.

Kolob Canyons Road
Kolob Arch
The Great White Throne
Zion Canyon Scenic Drive
Zion Canyon
Zion-Mount Carmel Highway
Zion Canyon Visitor Center
Checkerboard Mesa
0 km   9
0 miles   9
Virgin River

Ringtail   Mountain lion
Mule deer

Black visitors

Less than 5 percent of national park visitors are Black Americans. The "1 Million African American Youth In A Park" program was set up to encourage more young Black visitors to experience the beauty of Zion and other national parks.

Walter's Wiggles

In 1926, Zion's first superintendent, Walter Ruesch, carved a flight of 21 switchbacks in the steep cliffs of the park. This feature became known as Walter's Wiggles and is now a popular attraction.

Hoodoos vary in height from that of an average human to that exceeding a 10-story building.

Housing hoodoos

Bryce Canyon is not a single canyon at all but houses the world's biggest collection of rocky spires called hoodoos. The word "hoodoo" means "to bewitch"—visitors have been spellbound by this skyline since the park opened in 1928.

Bryce Canyon

UTAH

Just a short, scenic drive from Zion is Bryce Canyon. This national park is instantly recognizable for its unusual rock formations, called hoodoos. There are also stunning canyons to explore by day and starry skies to enjoy by night.

State Route 12

State Route 63

Visitor Center

Sunrise Pont

Bryce Amphitheater is full of hoodoo rocks.

N

Natural Bridge

Pink Cliffs

Rainbow Point

Steller's jay
Mule deer
Uinta chipmunk
Horned toad

0 km   5
0 miles   5

Busy burrows

Around 200 prairie dogs live in Bryce Canyon, sometimes darting about the meadows in the summer sunshine. These small, sociable rodents dig a maze of elaborate underground burrows, called "prairie dog towns."

Prairie dog stands alert to danger at a burrow entrance

Paintbrush plant

The Bryce Canyon paintbrush, which is only found locally and in some surrounding areas, grows to just 6 in (15 cm) tall. Despite its small size, it thrives because its roots absorb nutrients from nearby plants.

The colored leaves enclose the flower.

Starry nights

Bryce Canyon's clean air and elevated location combine to create some of the US's darkest night skies suitable for stargazing. Every summer, the park's four-day Astronomy Festival celebrates the constellations with telescope displays, guided tours, and guest speakers.

Grand Canyon

ARIZONA

Like a vast slash on Arizona's face, the nearly 1-mile- (1.6-km-) deep Grand Canyon stretches across an incredible 278 miles (447 km). For about six million years, its canyons and cliffs were gouged out of the ground by the Colorado River that snakes its way through this truly spectacular national park.

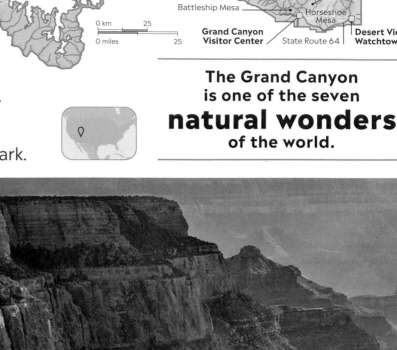

Kaibab squirrel
Grand Canyon rattlesnake
Rocky Mountain elk
Canyon wren
California condor
Bighorn sheep

Colorado River
State Route 67
Kaibab Plateau
Zoroaster Temple
Battleship Mesa
Horseshoe Mesa
Grand Canyon Visitor Center
State Route 64
Desert View Watchtower

0 km 25
0 miles 25

The Grand Canyon is one of the seven natural wonders of the world.

Majestic canyon

Sunlight reveals the steep-sided cliffs in a fiery display of rainbow rocks, showcasing the true beauty of the canyons. Seen in the distance is the mighty Colorado River as it winds its way across this magnificent landscape.

CREATING THE CANYON

Erosion by the Colorado River has created the Grand Canyon, which is layers of sedimentary rock—two-billion-year-old rock at the bottom and recent rock at the top. The Colorado River erodes 1 ft (0.3 m) of rocky layers through the center every 200 years.

The Colorado River cuts downward into the rock.

The canyon widens as the river reaches a layer of softer rocks.

The cliff collapses where the rock above loses support.

Colorado River

Starting in the Rocky Mountains, the Colorado River flows over 1,450 miles (2,330 km) before draining into the Gulf of California. Visitors can hire rafts and go whitewater rafting in the river

Lisa Hendy

Previously the first female chief ranger at Great Smoky Mountains National Park, Lisa Hendy now works as a district ranger in the Grand Canyon. She has won awards for her lifesaving achievements in the park.

Easy riders

Since the late 19th century, park visitors have enjoyed mule rides, whether along the top rim for panoramic views or deep inside the canyon to realize its sheer size. As the offspring of a horse and donkey, mules have plenty of strength and stamina.

Sturdy mules are sure-footed over the uneven canyon terrain.

Ancient land

Artifacts such as the ones on the right have been found in the Grand Canyon, which has been home to humans for more than 8,000 years. Today, about 11 tribes of Indigenous peoples, including the Havasupai, Hopi, Hualapai, and Kaibab Band of Paiute Indians, call this region their ancestral land.

Split-twig figurines, 6500–1250 BCE

Glow in the dark

The tiny bark scorpion glows under ultraviolet light in the canyon's darker reaches. This makes it easy for visitors to spot and avoid the painful sting in its tail!

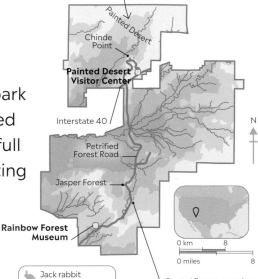
Details of the ancient tree bark are still visible in this petrified log.

Stony wood
Petrified wood is the official fossil of Arizona. It forms slowly over time where ancient trees fossilize into stone—they get buried in sediment before minerals dissolved in water replace the woody parts to form a stone replica.

Petrified Forest

ARIZONA

Named after some ancient coniferous trees that petrified (turned to stone), this unique national park contains one of the biggest collections of petrified wood anywhere on Earth. The Petrified Forest is full of spectacular sights and dinosaur fossils, attracting more than 600,000 visitors every year.

The Painted Desert is famous for its brightly colored rocky terrain.

Painted Desert

Chinde Point

Painted Desert Visitor Center

Interstate 40

Petrified Forest Road

Jasper Forest

N

Rainbow Forest Museum

0 km   8
0 miles   8

Crystal Forest contains petrified logs that glint in the sunlight.

- Jack rabbit
- Pronghorn
- Kit fox
- Great Plains toad

Two black stripes form a "collar" around the lizard's neck.

Rainbow reptile
The collared lizard stands out as the park's biggest lizard with striking colors. It lounges in the sun on petrified logs and bites if under attack.

FOSSILIZED FOREST

Millions of years ago, some dead trees were washed into rivers where they mixed with volcanic ash and sand in the water. They slowly turned from wood to stone, while preserving much of their original features.

1. Flooding
Floodwaters covered the base of the trees, uprooting many so they fell down.

2. Fossilization
Gradually over time, the trees became buried in ash and sand before turning to stone.

3. Erosion
Eventually the sand eroded to reveal the colorful petrified trunks in intricate detail.

Painted Desert
The vivid layers of the Painted Desert are produced by impurities in the almost solid quartz. Carbon, iron, and manganese give color to this otherwise barren and dry landscape.

Giant cactus

Reaching 50 ft (15 m) tall, saguaro is the US's biggest cactus and the undisputed symbol of the American West. Thousands of saguaros grow all over this national park, flowering during the summer months.

Saguaro
ARIZONA

Indigenous to this desert land, the super-sized saguaro cactus is the park's biggest attraction and gives it its name. Saguaro National Park is divided into two separate sections of east and west on either side of Tucson city.

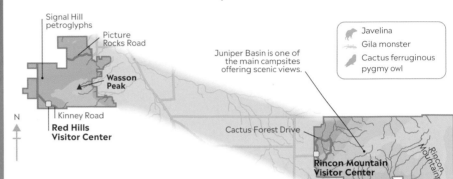

Signal Hill petroglyphs
Picture Rocks Road
Wasson Peak
Kinney Road
Red Hills Visitor Center
N
Juniper Basin is one of the main campsites offering scenic views.
Javelina
Gila monster
Cactus ferruginous pygmy owl
Cactus Forest Drive
Rincon Mountain Visitor Center
Rincon Mountains
0 km   8
0 miles   8

Bird's nest

The Gila woodpecker builds its nest inside the plentiful saguaros for safety and shade from the scorching sun. Both parents care for the young by foraging for vegetation and insects to bring home.

Blazing a trail

Park trails range from easy forest walks to steep mountain climbs. It is essential to carry water and hike around dawn or dusk to avoid the soaring temperatures.

Old petroglyphs

Rock carvings discovered in the west of Saguaro were created by the Hohokam people. Called petroglyphs, they depict different patterns with meanings that are not fully understood.

Joshua Tree
CALIFORNIA

Two dramatic desert landscapes meet at the Joshua Tree National Park. The lower Colorado Desert is dotted with cactus plants and creosote bush, while the upper Mojave Desert is home to the unique Joshua trees that give the park its name.

Old pictographs

The park was home to different Indigenous peoples, including the Pinto, Serrano, Chemehuevi, and Cahuilla. They left their mark on the rocks, creating petroglyphs (design carved into rock) and pictographs (paintings on rocks).

Bighorn sheep	Roadrunner
Coyote	Rosy boa

Map labels:
- Black Rock Campground
- Park Boulevard
- Oasis Visitor Center
- Oasis of Mara
- Barker Dam
- Covington Flat
- Pinto Basin Road
- Cholla Cactus Garden
- Cottonwood Spring Oasis
- 0 km 15
- 0 miles 15
- N

Joshua trees

Spiky silhouettes of Joshua trees—which are a type of yucca plant—stand out against the sparse skyline. The tree was named after a biblical leader Joshua as it reminded early Mormon settlers in the area of the hero raising his outstretched arms toward the heavens.

Honeypot ants

Life is tough in the desert and only the strongest survive. Honeypot ants eat as much honey as they can to help the colony. Some of them become living jars of honey ready for other ants to feed from them.

Abdomen is full to bursting with honey for the ant colony.

Spiky leaves minimize water loss.

Giant boulders make this national park a popular playground for climbers.

Channel Islands

CALIFORNIA

In an idyllic setting off the California coastline, Channel Islands National Park stretches over a chain of five rugged islands surrounded by ocean. The protected waters are home to many aquatic species supported by underwater kelp forests.

Marine mammals

San Miguel Island hosts one of the world's biggest populations of sea lions, which swim near the shores of the neighboring islands. About 80,000 of these marine mammals breed on San Miguel's rocky outcrops in the Pacific Ocean.

The Robert J. Lagomarsino Visitor Center

Prisoners Harbour

Santa Cruz Island

Anacapa Island

San Miguel Island

Santa Rosa Island

0 km   20
0 miles   20

Santa Cruz Island is the largest of the Channel Islands and home to the Santa Cruz Island fox.

N

Santa Barbara Island

Legend:
- Sea lion
- California brown pelican
- Deer mouse
- Spotted skunk
- Santa Cruz Island fox

Island chain

From Inspiration Point on Anacapa Island, visitors can see the neighboring islands of Santa Cruz, Santa Rosa, and San Miguel in clear view. The Channel Islands were formed by the Pacific tectonic plate and the North American continent moving together.

Pinnacles

CALIFORNIA

The unique landscape of this region formed from erupting volcanoes and lava flow. In 2013, Pinnacles National Park opened for visitors to view the towering rocks, canyon caves, and the nation's biggest birds.

California condor

The endangered California condor is the US's largest flying bird. It nearly became extinct in 1987 because of human activity. Today, Pinnacles is the only national park where condors are bred in captivity to increase their numbers.

Wingspan measures 10 ft (3 m)

Stone spires

Pinnacles is named after its lofty spiral peaks, shaped slowly over time by volcanic activity coupled with wind and water erosion. There are also domed rocks and bat caves attracting climbers and hikers.

N

State Route 146

East Entrance

Pinnacles Visitor Center

High Peaks

Gabilan Range

Bear Gulch Reservoir

Pinnacles Campground

West Entrance
State Route 146

0 km   1
0 miles   1

Legend:
- Townsend's big-eared bat
- Red-legged frog
- Prairie falcon

Lowest point

Located 282 ft (86 m) below sea level, Badwater Basin is the lowest point in the US. This huge expanse of salt flats creates a dazzling white sheen. In addition to sodium chloride (common salt), other minerals found on the flats include calcite, gypsum, and borax.

Death Valley
CALIFORNIA

Welcome to the hottest and driest national park in the US. This extreme region in the Mojave Desert was given its name by the 19th-century settlers who found the valley difficult to cross and feared they would perish in the scorching sun and remote terrain.

Venomous viper

The Mojave rattlesnake lives in the southern desert and mountains of Death Valley. It is one of the most venomous snakes in the US. This nocturnal viper avoids the relentless heat of the day by laying low under rocks or in burrows.

The rattle at the end of the tail is made up of loose rings of hard, dry skin.

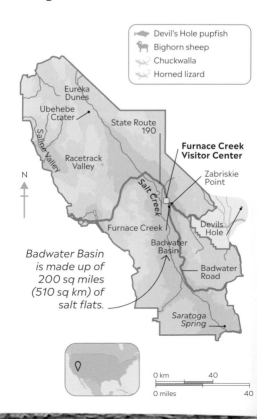

- Devil's Hole pupfish
- Bighorn sheep
- Chuckwalla
- Horned lizard

Eureka Dunes
Ubehebe Crater
Saline Valley
State Route 190
Furnace Creek Visitor Center
Racetrack Valley
Zabriskie Point
Salt Creek
N
Furnace Creek
Devils Hole
Badwater Basin
Badwater Road

Badwater Basin is made up of 200 sq miles (510 sq km) of salt flats.

Saratoga Spring

0 km — 40
0 miles — 40

In 1913, temperatures in Death Valley soared to a record-setting
134°F (57°C).

Each wagon weighed about 7,800 lb (3,500 kg) and could carry up to 10 tons of borax.

Bringing borax

In the late 19th century, the mineral borax was used for cleaning, cosmetics, and even medicine. When large quantities were found in Death Valley, borax began to be transported to the nearest railroads by mule-pulled wagons.

Sailing stones

Mystery once surrounded the sailing stones, rocks that appeared to move across the desert without any explanation. However, in 2014, experts discovered that whenever rainwater froze overnight, ice formed across the desert floor. When blown by heavy winds, these ice sheets would move, pushing the rocks.

👁 EYEWITNESS

Justin Stroup

Justin Stroup is one of several researchers studying water levels over the last 200,000 years in Death Valley and Searles Basin in California. In the past, Death Valley had large lakes, so his research is helping to understand the impact of climate change over time.

Put the kettle on!

The sign for Teakettle Junction in Death Valley is covered in kettles—containing handwritten messages—left by travelers. This decades-old tradition is said to bring good luck.

Sequoia and Kings Canyon

CALIFORNIA

Despite being administered as one unit, Sequoia and Kings Canyon National Parks are each unique. Sequoia, which has towering trees and granite domes, is easily accessible with short hikes, whereas Kings Canyon features waterfalls, rivers, and meadows, and is sprawling rugged wilderness.

Super sequoia

Meet General Sherman, the largest tree by volume on Earth. More than 2,000 years old, this giant sequoia tree stands 275 ft (83 m) tall and 100 ft (30 m) around the base—a true test for tree-huggers in this national park!

Managing wildfires

California wildfires are increasing in number, with about 15 giant sequoia groves affected here. The National Park Service manages this threat by increasing park ranger staff and air emergency services (above) and educating visitors on fire safety.

Kings Canyon is deeper than the Grand Canyon.

Kings River

Kings Canyon

KINGS CANYON NATIONAL PARK

The General Grant Tree

Redwood Mountain Grove

Kings Canyon Scenic Byway

Grant Grove Visitor Center

Muir Grove

General Sherman Tree

Giant Forest

Generals Highway

SEQUOIA NATIONAL PARK

Kern River

Foothills Visitor Center

Kaweah River

- Mountain lion
- Black bear
- King snake
- Alpine chipmunk
- Prairie falcon

Granite cliffs exposed beneath the snow-covered slopes

On the trail

Kings Canyon has an extensive range of hiking trails that lead to the most remote terrain. Intrepid explorers are rewarded with staggering views of the Sierra Nevada mountain range, alpine lakes, and plentiful wildlife.

The frogs can grow up to 3.5 in (8.9 cm) long.

Endangered frog

The mountain yellow-legged frog lives in these parks. The introduction of fish that prey on it has caused a decline in its population. Conservation efforts are now targeting this animal's dwindling numbers

Great Basin

NEVADA

By day, Great Basin reveals one of the most mountainous regions in the US, as well as alpine forests, limestone caverns, and glacial lakes. By night, the dark skies light up in a celestial show for stargazers. Unusually, the water in this region drains inward instead of flowing to the ocean.

Adventure park

Widespread trails, extensive hikes, and overnight camping mean endless opportunities for exploring the park. The greatest challenge for climbers is scaling the 13,065 ft (3,982 m) high Wheeler Peak.

Lehman Cave

Named after the rancher Absalom Lehman, who discovered this limestone cavern in the 1880s, the Lehman Cave features at least 500 unique calcite shield formations and countless stalactites and stalagmites.

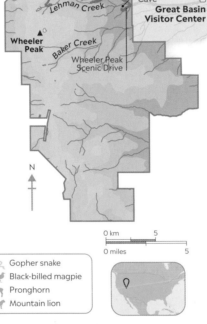

Lehman Creek

Lehman Cave

Great Basin Visitor Center

Wheeler Peak

Baker Creek

Wheeler Peak Scenic Drive

N

0 km 5
0 miles 5

Gopher snake
Black-billed magpie
Pronghorn
Mountain lion

Timeless tree

Among the world's oldest species of tree, the Great Basin bristlecone pine grows at high altitude and in freezing temperatures where few plants can survive. High winds twist the trunks of these slow growers into unique shapes.

Night train

All aboard! The Great Basin Star Train offers guided tours of the starry skies on summer nights. This remote area is known for its exceptional stargazing and is a certified International Dark Sky Park.

Yosemite
CALIFORNIA

The spectacular setting of this national park in the Sierra Nevada mountains is known for its rushing waterfalls, ancient granite cliffs, forested valleys, lush meadows, and towering sequoia trees. Yosemite is home to a range of animals, from butterflies to bears.

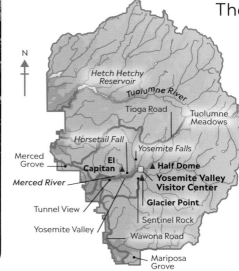

0 km   15
0 miles   15

N

Hetch Hetchy Reservoir
Tuolumne River
Tioga Road
Tuolumne Meadows
Horsetail Fall
Yosemite Falls
Merced Grove
El Capitan
▲ Half Dome
Yosemite Valley Visitor Center
Merced River
Glacier Point
Tunnel View
Sentinel Rock
Yosemite Valley
Wawona Road
Mariposa Grove

Firefall

A rare but remarkable phenomenon can occur during winter sunsets at Horsetail Fall when the waterfall reflects the fading sunlight like falling fire. This waterfall is not as big as nearby Yosemite Falls, which is one of the nation's tallest waterfalls.

Red fox
Sierra Nevada bighorn sheep
Pacific fisher
Mountain lion

Red bear road signs remind drivers to drive slowly in black bear country.

Red bear

In 2007, Yosemite created the "Red Bear, Dead Bear" campaign to encourage safe driving and raise awareness of the American black bears living in the park. Sign posts mark places where bears have been hit and killed on park roads.

Granite surface is smooth and slippery, resulting in a difficult climb.

Inspired by Yosemite's beauty, a visitor paints a scene at a workshop.

Art in the park

The natural beauty of Yosemite has inspired all kinds of artists, including Thomas Ayres, who drew the first published illustration of the Yosemite Valley in the 1800s. Today, visitors can enjoy many creative workshops at the park. Since 1983, the park's administration has run art programs that allow guests to connect with nature in a new way.

Two metal cables help the hikers during the final part of the ascent.

El Capitan   *Half Dome*

View of El Capitan and Half Dome from Tunnel View

Half Dome was thought to be inaccessible because of its steep rock face until it was first climbed in 1875

Challenging climb

At a height of nearly 8,800 ft (2,680 m), Half Dome is a giant granite rock formation that is scaled by 50,000 hikers every year. However, the steep climbs and sheer drops mean it is not suitable for beginners. Hikers need experience and special permission for it.

Lassen Volcanic
CALIFORNIA

Northern California's Lassen Volcanic features all kinds of volcanoes, steaming hot springs, and bubbling mud spots. Shimmering lakes, sun-dappled forests, and meadows laden with wildflowers add to its beauty.

Volcanic view

At 10,457 ft (3,187 m), Lassen Peak is the world's largest dome volcano. The summit offers unparalleled views of Lake Helen, a glacial lake that reflects the volcano in its blue waters.

Clark's nutcracker
Douglas squirrel
Sierra Nevada red fox

Loomis Plaza
Cinder Cone ▲
Fantastic Lava Beds
Lassen Peak Highway
Emerald Lake
▲ Lassen Peak
Lake Helen
Bumpass Hell
Sulphur Works
Kings Creek
Kohm Yah-mah-nee

N

0 km 7
0 miles 7

Frog chorus

The Pacific tree frog's unique high-pitched call can be heard in a lively frog chorus after dark. It is one of six amphibians living near water sources in the national park.

Hot as hell

Past volcanic activity has left its mark on the area called Bumpass Hell. Here, visitors can walk past hot springs, mud pools, and fumaroles (openings in the ground that let out volcanic gases and vapor).

Crater Lake
OREGON

At the heart of this national park is Crater Lake, the deepest lake in the US, which plunges to depths of nearly 2,000 ft (600 m). Its picture-perfect location is surrounded by the evergreen forests of the Cascade Mountains.

Rim riders

Visitors can rent bicycles and ride around the entire rim of the lake. This trip of 33 miles (53 km) is rewarded with breathtaking panoramic views.

True blue

Almost 8,000 years ago, Mount Mazama erupted and its peak collapsed inward, leaving behind a crater that filled with water to form Crater Lake. Today, its vivid blue waters attract photographers, artists, and thrill-seekers.

0 km 8
0 miles 8

N

North Entrance Road
Wizard Island
Rim Drive
Crater Lake
Rim Village Visitor Center
Mount Scott
Crater Lake Highway
Phantom Ship
Volcanic Legacy Scenic Byway

Snowshoe hare
Northern flying squirrel
Crater Lake newt
Boreal toad

Huge hug

Tree huggers face their greatest challenge yet in stretching their arms around the coast redwoods! The thickest trees have taken as long as 2,000 years to spread 20 ft (6 m) wide.

Redwood
CALIFORNIA

The tallest trees on Earth have grown to record-breaking heights at Redwood National Park over many centuries. Giant redwoods dominate the landscape, which varies between ancient woodland, open prairies, and rocky coastline.

RECORD-BREAKING REDWOODS

Coast redwoods are the tallest living things on Earth, growing to heights of nearly 390 ft (120 m). Hyperion, the tallest redwood and tree in the world, is 1.25 times taller than the Statue of Liberty.

Hyperion	Helios	Nugget
(380.8 ft/ 116.1 m)	(377.1 ft/ 114.9 m)	(373.5 ft/ 113.8 m)

JEDEDIAH SMITH REDWOODS STATE PARK

Crescent City Information Center

Crescent Beach

Highway 101

DEL NORTE COAST REDWOODS STATE PARK

PRAIRIE CREEK REDWOODS STATE PARK

Newton B. Drury Scenic Parkway

Orick Ranger Station

N

Tall Trees Grove

0 km — 13
0 miles — 13

- Sea lion
- Sea otter
- Roosevelt elk
- Gray whale

THAT'S A BIG TREE!

BIGGER TREES

THAT'S A VERY BIG TREE!

THE "BIG TREE"

THIS WAY TO MORE BIG TREES!

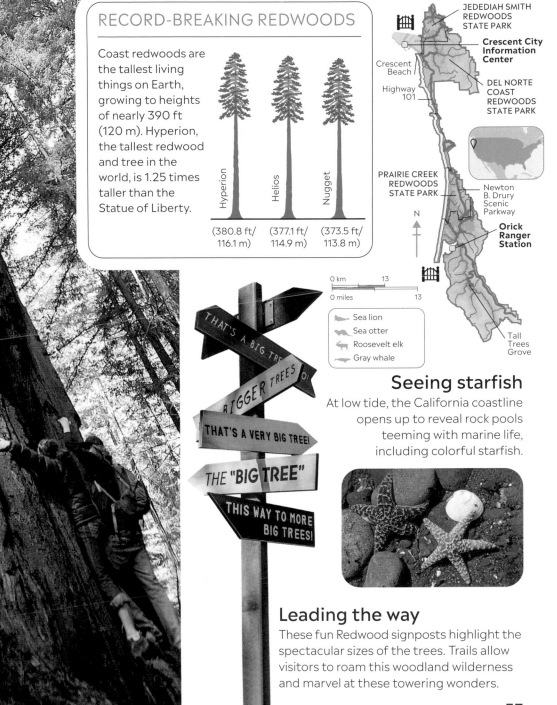

Seeing starfish

At low tide, the California coastline opens up to reveal rock pools teeming with marine life, including colorful starfish.

Leading the way

These fun Redwood signposts highlight the spectacular sizes of the trees. Trails allow visitors to roam this woodland wilderness and marvel at these towering wonders.

Mount Rainier
WASHINGTON

Against the impressive backdrop of Mount Rainier is a park famed for thriving flora and fauna, as well as its use of "parkitecture"—human-made structures built from local materials that blend with the environment.

Record-breaker Rainier

Mount Rainier stands tall at 14,409 ft (4,392 m). Hikers can head to the top on a summit adventure, hit the slopes on a hiking trail, or lay low enjoying the wildflower meadows.

0 km 10
0 miles 10

Bobcat
Spotted owl
Mountain goat

Carbon River
Mather Memorial Parkway
N
▲ Carbon Glacier
Mount Rainier ▲
▲ Emmons Glacier
▲ Paradise Glacier
Henry M Jackson Memorial Visitor Center
Reflection Lakes
Nisqually River
Narada Falls
Stevens Canyon Road
Ohanapecosh Visitor Center

Take the plunge

Close to the Paradise Visitor Center is a glorious photo opportunity at Narada Falls. The waters plunge 188 ft (57 m) over two tiers of steep rock.

Trusted trout

Bull trout have nine crystal-clear mountain rivers to swim. This fish has been an important source of food for Indigenous peoples for thousands of years.

North Cascades
WASHINGTON

Named after its many cascading waterfalls, North Cascades has rugged peaks, forested valleys, and over 300 glaciers—more than enough for hikers and campers to enjoy.

Ross Lake
▲ **Mount Shuksan**
N
North Cascades Visitor Center
Skagit River
North Cascades Scenic Highway
Stehekin River

0 km 20
0 miles 20

Diablo Lake is a favorite spot for kayaking and canoeing.

Goode Mountain
Lake Chelan

Canada lynx
River otter
Osprey
Black-tailed deer
Mountain goat

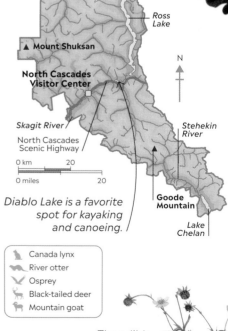

Eagle eyes

Bald eagles fly from Canada and Alaska to the North Cascades in the winter when salmon spawn. Most of them arrive at Skagit River.

Big blue

Visitors are attracted to Diablo Lake's turquoise blue waters. Tiny particles from glacial rock refract the sun's rays to produce this incredible color.

The edible fruits of this plant are brightly colored.

Protecting plants

Many local plants are vulnerable to damage from passing hikers. Park rangers now grow many of these plants, such as this wild strawberry, outside the park before reintroducing them inside it.

Olympic
WASHINGTON

Thanks to its incredibly diverse terrain, Olympic is known as three parks in one—with distinct regions of alpine mountains, evergreen forests, and rugged coastline.

Camping on the beach

Camping is permitted on the unspoiled Pacific beaches. Nature has made its mark along this coastline with sea stacks, driftwood deposits, and rock pools.

Hoh Rain Forest is named after the Hoh River.

Route 101

Lake Crescent

Olympic National Park Visitor Center

Upper Hoh Road

Sol Duc

Hoh Rain Forest

Hurricane Ridge

▲ Mount Olympus

0 km 20
0 miles 20

Quinault Rain Forest

N

Huge antlers of male elk grow back every summer.

Bald eagle
Roosevelt elk
Ochre sea stars
Olympic marmot
Black oystercatcher

👁 EYEWITNESS

Gordon Hempton
For 40 years, Gordon Hempton has recorded sounds of nature, including the deep hum inside a Sitka spruce log at Olympic. His recordings reveal how the quiet places on Earth are being increasingly polluted by human-made noise.

Going green

The Hoh Rain Forest is one of the US's biggest temperate rainforests, with spruce, cedar, maple, and hemlock trees providing a leafy green sanctuary for all kinds of wildlife.

Roaming Roosevelt

The largest herd of Roosevelt elk in the Pacific Northwest lives at Olympic. Their name comes from President Theodore Roosevelt who established the park mainly as an elk reserve.

Slug life

Indigenous to the Pacific Northwest, the banana slug resembles the fruit it is named after. With a maximum speed of 6.5 in (16.5 cm) per minute, it is one of the world's slowest movers.

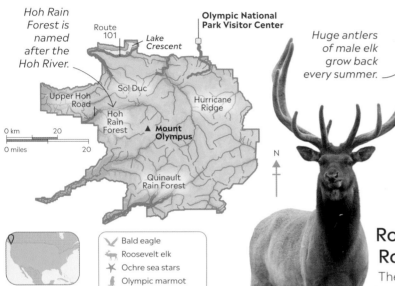

Steller sea lion
The park is a haven for marine life, including Steller (or northern) sea lions breeding along the coastline. Massive males can weigh up to a staggering 2,500 lb (1,100 kg), while females weigh up to 800 lb (360 kg).

Forming icebergs
There are nearly 1,000 glaciers in this national park. Common to the ones on the coastline is calving—the process of a large piece of ice breaking off and splashing into the sea as an iceberg.

Glacier Bay covers 3.3 million acres (1.3 million ha) of land and water.

Glacier Bay
ALASKA

Visited most easily by boat, this world heritage site in southeast Alaska is spectacular from land and sea. On land, there are rugged mountain peaks, dense forests, and giant glaciers, while one-fifth of the park is marine water.

Muir Glacier

Fairweather Range

Chilkat Range

Bartlett Cove

Glacier Bay Lodge Visitor Center

0 km 40
0 miles 40

Salmon represents foresight, trust, and rebirth.

Orca
Humpback whale
Horned puffin

Tlingit culture
Glacier Bay is home to the Tlingit people who have lived off the land for centuries. This Tlingit Totem Pole celebrates a new friendship formed between these people and the park authorities.

Wrangell-St. Elias
ALASKA

The US's largest national park, Wrangell-St. Elias covers more than 13 million acres (5 million hectares). It has a changing and varied landscape, from mountains and glaciers to forests and rivers.

0 km 100
0 miles 100

Copper Center Visitor Center
Copper River
Wrangell Mountains
Mount Wrangell
Root Glacier Trail
Kennicott Glacier
Kennecott Mines
McCarthy Road
St. Elias Mountains

The Bagley Icefield is North America's second-largest icefield.

Hubbard Glacier

N

Abandoned mines
In the 19th-century, copper ore was discovered in the Kennecott wilderness. The Kennecott mines were built to extract this ore. The site was named a National Historic Landmark in 1986.

Dall sheep
Iceworm
Harbor seal
Ptarmigan
Wolverine

Exploring glaciers
Adventurers are spoiled for choice with many mountains to climb and glaciers to explore. Expert climbers use tools such as ice axes to carefully move along vertical routes. Traveling with a guide is recommended.

Kenai Fjords

ALASKA

In 1980, Kenai Fjords was established to protect some of Alaska's most remote wilderness. The park is named after the many fjords (long bodies of water stretching inland) formed from the movement of glaciers.

Exit Glacier

Ressurection Bay

Harding Icefield is among the largest in the US.

Kenai Fjords National Park Visitor Center

N

Porcupine Bay

McCarty Fjord

Aialik Bay

Gulf of Alaska

Iceworm
Mountain goat
Sea lion
Black bear

0 km 20
0 miles 20

Whale of a time!

Kenai Fjords is one of the best places in Alaska to go whale watching. Orcas and humpback whales are most likely to be spotted on boat trips from March to October.

Sea stacks

Rushing winds, crashing waves, and daily tides erode the rocky coastline, forming sea caves and arches. As erosion continues, the arches lose their roof, leaving sea stacks standing tall in the water.

Katmai

ALASKA

There are few places on Earth with more volcanic activity than Katmai, a sprawling wilderness shaped by countless volcanic eruptions. The national park is dotted with 14 active volcanoes today.

King Salmon Visitor Center

Alagnak River

Naknek Lake

Brooks Falls

Brooks River

Valley of Ten Thousand Smokes

Novarupta-Katmai

N

0 km 50
0 miles 50

Brown bear
Sea otter
Sockeye salmon
Red fox
Bald eagle

Fishing bears

Every year, schools of sockeye salmon return from the Pacific to the rivers where they hatched before laying their eggs. This salmon run attracts 2,000 brown bears to Katmai, with a grand ending at Brooks Falls.

Caldera lake

The lake atop Mount Katmai resembles a bubbling blue cauldron with a rim. Mount Katmai is an active volcano that erupted in 1912 before its top collapsed. This left behind a depression, called a caldera, that has now filled up with water.

The caldera lake is more than 800 ft (250 m) deep.

Denali
ALASKA

At Denali, snowcapped mountains tower over an alpine tundra landscape criss-crossed by braided rivers. There is only one established roadway in the park, which was the first one in the US to protect wildlife habitats. It is home to many large mammals, including grizzly bears, wolves, and moose.

At 20,310 ft (6,190 m), Mount Denali is the **tallest mountain** in North America.

Protective clothing is essential in the Alaskan wilderness.

Indigenous name

Hiking in the wilderness gives uninterrupted views of Mount Denali. It was previously known as Mount McKinley, but in 2016, its original Alaskan name was restored. Denali means "the tall one," in the language of the Indigenous Athabascan people.

PERMAFROST

Any ground that stays frozen below 32°F (0°C) for two or more years is called permafrost, but the soil above it may thaw each year under the summer sun. About 45 percent of Denali has continuous permafrost, which stops plant roots from growing deep, limiting their height above ground.

The layer above permafrost thaws in summer and freezes in winter.

The ground below can be unfrozen.

Permafrost is made of ice, sand, rock, and gravel.

Chilchukabena Lake
East Fork Toklat River
Old Cache Lake
Teklanika River
Toklat River
McKinley River
Denali Park Road
Igloo Mountain ▲
Riley Creek
Kantishna Roadhouse ☐
Wonder Lake
▲ Eielson Visitor Center ☐
▲ Mount Eielson
Muldrow Glacier ▲
Peters Glacier ▲
▲ Mount Brooks
Kahiltna Dome ▲
▲ Mount Denali
Mount ▲ Foraker
▲ Mount Frances
▲ Ruth Glacier

N

Gray wolf	Moose
Caribou	Black bear
Brown bear	Dall sheep

Kahiltna is the longest glacier in the Alaska Range.

0 km   30
0 miles   30

Leighan Falley

Alaskan bush pilot Leighan Falley has clocked 4,000 hours in the air during her flying career. She is the main subject of *Denali's Raven*, a 2017 documentary that describes her experience as a national park bush pilot, including emergency rescues, air taxi services, and aerial sightseeing tours.

Pulling sleds

Dashing through the snow in a sled pulled by huskies is one of the most popular visitor activities in Denali—the only US national park with working sled dogs. Alaskan huskies have the strength and stamina to pull sleds at high speed during the winter season, when teams of rangers and dogs set off to patrol the Denali wilderness.

A measuring ruler gives a clear idea of the size of this fossilized footprint.

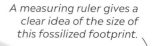

Fossil finds

Denali is positioned on the 70-million-year-old Cantwell Formation, an area rich in dinosaur tracks and bones. A 2016 scientific expedition to Denali revealed the discovery of an almost perfectly preserved footprint belonging to a meat-eating dinosaur.

Sky lights

On the top of most people's bucket list is the Aurora Borealis, or Northern Lights. During the winter months, there is a good chance of seeing this natural light show over Denali.

Lake Clark

ALASKA

The remote wilderness of Alaska is home to one of the country's least visited national parks. Lake Clark is a hidden gem bursting with craggy mountains, tranquil lakes, and a wide range of wildlife.

Still waters

Surrounded by breathtaking mountains, Lake Clark is the jumping off point to outdoor activities in the national park. With no roads leading to it, nature lovers, kayakers, and anglers can reach this lake by seaplane or bush plane.

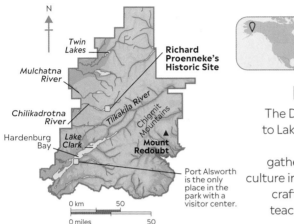

Twin Lakes

Richard Proenneke's Historic Site

Mulchatna River

Chilikadrotna River

Tlikakila River

Hardenburg Bay

Lake Clark

Chigmit Mountains

Mount Redoubt

Port Alsworth is the only place in the park with a visitor center.

0 km 50

0 miles 50

Gray wolf
Caribou
Sea otter
Beluga whale
Brown bear

Dena'ina homeland

The Dena'ina people have lived close to Lake Clark for at least 10,000 years, surviving on fishing, hunting, and gathering food. Today, they carry their culture into the future through traditional crafts, sustainability practices, and by teaching visitors about their heritage.

Sands of time

It is rare to find dunes in the Arctic, yet Kobuk Valley has three major dune fields—slowly carved by glaciers over thousands of years. Life thrives here, with muskox and caribou leaving their footprints in the sand.

Kobuk Valley

ALASKA

Boreal forests and crystal-clear rivers pepper Kobuk's dramatic tundra landscape, which sits entirely north of the Arctic Circle. This remote valley is best explored with a guide.

Baird Mountains

Salmon River

Northwest Arctic Heritage Center

Hunt River Dunes

Onion Portage

Great Kobuk Sand Dunes

Kobuk River

Little Kobuk Sand Dunes

0 km 20

0 miles 20

Caribou
Muskox
Canada lynx
Sockeye salmon
Arctic warbler

Caribou crossing

In one of the world's largest mammal migrations, up to 250,000 caribou travel in huge herds across the Kobuk Valley twice a year to reach their breeding grounds.

Both male and female caribou have antlers, which they use to protect their food and territory.

Open gates

Of the few named landmarks in this remote landscape, the Boreal Mountain and Frigid Crags create a natural entrance to this national park. The "Gates" were named by American conservationist Robert Marshall who traveled here during the 1930s.

Gates of the Arctic

ALASKA

Almost entirely untouched, Gates of the Arctic National Park has no established roads, trails, or campsites. It is a true wilderness and welcomes only a few thousand visitors a year.

Ice-age survivor

The muskox has evolved little since the last ice age when it migrated over the Bering Land Bridge that linked Asia and North America about 100,000 years ago. Muskox are still covered in shaggy fur, helping them to survive the frozen Arctic climate.

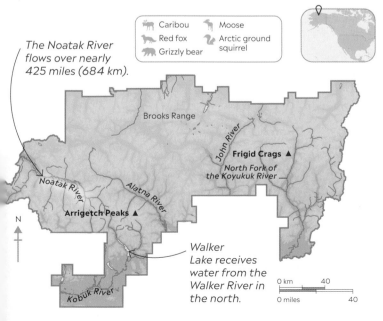

The Noatak River flows over nearly 425 miles (684 km).

Caribou
Red fox
Grizzly bear
Moose
Arctic ground squirrel

Brooks Range

John River

Frigid Crags ▲

North Fork of the Koyukuk River

Noatak River

Alatna River

Arrigetch Peaks ▲

Walker Lake receives water from the Walker River in the north.

Kobuk River

N

0 km 40
0 miles 40

Wild rivers

The six wild rivers in the park mark historical travel routes for Indigenous Alaskan peoples. Today, these protected waters are a lifeline for wildlife, as well as a playground for paddlers.

American Samoa

Spread over three beautiful islands—Tutuila, Ofu, and Ta'ū—the National Park of American Samoa is a winning combination of sandy beaches, coral reefs, and tropical rainforests. In 1993, Samoan chiefs granted a special 50-year lease for the National Park Service to preserve and protect their stunning landscape and cultural heritage.

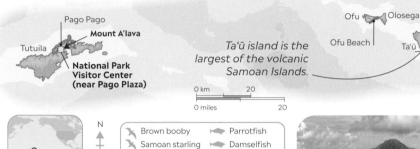

Pago Pago
Mount A'lava
Tutuila
National Park Visitor Center (near Pago Plaza)

Ta'ū island is the largest of the volcanic Samoan Islands.

Ofu — Olosega
Ofu Beach
Ta'ū

0 km   20
0 miles   20

N

Brown booby   Parrotfish
Samoan starling   Damselfish
Green sea turtle

Flying fox

Native to American Samoa, the Samoan flying fox is a fruit bat that feasts on tropical fruits. It can be spotted hanging from trees and flying through the rainforest.

Wingspan up to 3 ft (0.9 m)

View from Mount Tumu, Ofu

Tapa tradition

Samoa has been inhabited for 3,000 years and is steeped in ancient traditions. Samoans still fashion the bark of paper mulberry trees into tapa cloth, a handcrafted material used for many purposes, including clothing and ceremonies.

Coral reefs

The park protects 2,550 acres (1,030 ha) of coral reefs. The islands of Ofu and Olosega are popular for their white coral beaches and pristine reefs teeming with marine life. Snorkeling and diving are the easiest ways to experience this unspoiled underwater world.

Goose on the loose

Nēnē is the state bird of Hawai'i and the world's rarest goose. It nests on the Haleakalā volcano, using its webbed feet to navigate the treacherous terrain formed by solidified lava flows.

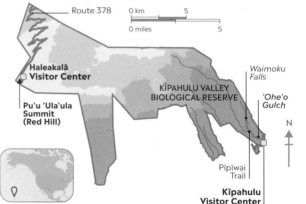

Nēnē is a medium-sized goose with brown and black plumes.

Haleakalā

HAWAI'I

Located on the Hawai'ian island of Maui, Haleakalā National Park is divided into two parts: the northwest is defined by its colorful volcanic landscape, while the southeast has black sand beaches along the coast and bamboo forest. Visitors enjoy the park's many attractions—from beautiful plants and birds to waterfalls and hiking trails.

- Hawai'ian petrel
- 'Apapane
- Hawai'ian wolf spider
- Hawai'ian hoary bat
- Western yellowjacket

Route 378

0 km   5
0 miles   5

Haleakalā Visitor Center

Pu'u 'Ula'ula Summit (Red Hill)

KĪPAHULU VALLEY BIOLOGICAL RESERVE

Waimoku Falls

'Ohe'o Gulch

N

Pīpīwai Trail

Kīpahulu Visitor Center

Top spot

Towering about 10,000 ft (3,000 m) above sea level, the summit of Haleakalā is the highest point on Maui. Breathtaking views, crater hikes, and a volcanic landscape attract visitors.

Giant grass

The Pīpīwai Trail in the Kīpahulu District is a glorious hike through bamboo forest with many photo opportunities. Bamboo was introduced by Polynesian explorers who used this tough, tropical grass to light fires, hold water, and craft tools.

Hawai'i Volcanoes

HAWAI'I

Seen on this hot spot of volcanic activity on Hawai'i's Big Island are ashen deserts, a lava-lined coastline, and many giant volcanoes—including the summits of Mount Kīlauea and Mauna Loa, two of the world's most active volcanoes.

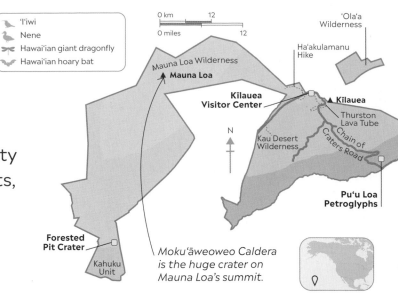

- 'I'iwi
- Nene
- Hawai'ian giant dragonfly
- Hawai'ian hoary bat

0 km 12
0 miles 12

'Ola'a Wilderness

Mauna Loa Wilderness

Ha'akulamanu Hike

▲ Mauna Loa

Kīlauea Visitor Center

▲ Kīlauea

Thurston Lava Tube

N

Kau Desert Wilderness

Chain of Craters Road

Pu'u Loa Petroglyphs

Forested Pit Crater

Kahuku Unit

Moku'āweoweo Caldera is the huge crater on Mauna Loa's summit.

Mega mountain

Mauna Loa is the largest active volcano on Earth. Measured from its base on the seabed to the gaping summit, it stands 30,000 ft (9,144 m), which easily beats Mount Everest.

'Ōhi'a lehua flowers usually bloom bright red but can also be pink, yellow, or white.

Prime plant

Found only in Hawai'i, the 'ōhi'a lehua plant is featured in many local legends. Historically, it has been used in ancient medicine for pain relief, as well as providing a vital source of nectar for island birds.

Park rangers give organized walking tours of the area.

Madame Pele

According to Hawai'ian legend, the goddess of volcanoes and fire, Pele, lives inside Mount Kīlauea and created Hawai'i's dramatic volcanic landscapes. It is said that visitors should ask Pele for permission to travel through her land—and never take a lava rock because they will be cursed!

Ha'akulamanu hike

The Ha'akulamanu trail is a short loop around the park, rewarded with incredible signs of geothermal activity. Steaming hot vents and rainbow mineral deposits are on view, while the air has traces of hydrogen sulfide—a gas that smells like rotten eggs.

Struggle for survival

The Hawai'ian hawksbill turtle is protected in the park waters. Females come to shore to nest, but only one in every 1,000 hatchlings survives to adulthood.

Endless eruption

Searing lava from Mount Kīlauea flows into the Pacific waters off Hawai'i's Big Island. The most active shield volcano in Hawai'i, Mount Kīlauea has been erupting continually since 1983. Fast-flowing, fiery lava from it lights up the landscape, reaching temperatures of 2,138°F (1,170°C). On cooling down, it hardens into solid layers of volcanic rock.

Mount Kīlauea is the world's
youngest volcano.

Find out more

There is no better way to understand the wonder of the national parks than to visit them. These dramatic landscapes are full of history, bursting with wildlife, and hold all kinds of records. You'll learn so much by reading this book and checking out the park map (see pp.6–7), then go online to prepare the finer details of your trip.

FAST FACTS

HIGHEST FALLS
With water tumbling from a height of 2,425 ft (739 m), Yosemite Falls in Yosemite National Park is the tallest waterfall in North America.

AMONG THE ARCHES
With more than 2,000 natural arches, Arches National Park has more arches than anywhere else in the world.

MONSTER ICEFIELD
Measuring 127 miles (204 km) long, Bagley icefield in Wrangell-St. Elias National Park is one of the biggest icefields in North America outside of the polar regions.

DUNE GIANT
Stretching 741 ft (225 m) from top to bottom, Star Dune at Great Sand Dunes National Park is the tallest dune in North America.

NATIONAL PRESERVES

National preserves are protected spaces that allow long-standing, local communities to continue hunting and fishing. In total, eight national parks are paired with a preserve. Six are in the remote wilderness of Alaska. The others are Great Sand Dunes in Colorado and New River Gorge in West Virginia.

Big and small

North America's national parks vary dramatically in size. The biggest and smallest parks are shown here. Wrangell-St. Elias National Park is a sprawling wilderness encompassing four mountain ranges, while Gateway Arch is named after its monumental arch and covers a much smaller scale.

Gateway Arch
192 acres
(77.7 ha)

Death Valley
3.3 million acres (1.3 million ha)

Katmai 4.1 million acres (1.7 million ha)

Denali 6.1 million acres (2.5 million ha)

Wrangell St. Elias 13.2 million acres (5.3 million ha)

This park is a whopping 68,000 times larger than Gateway Arch.

Great Smoky Mountains (14 million)

Zion (5 million)

Yellowstone (4.9 million)

Grand Canyon (4.5 million)

Rocky Mountain (4.4 million)

Approximate numbers of visitors to the national parks in 2021

Popular parks

In 2021, nearly 92 million visitors enjoyed the US national parks. Among the parks, five received the most visitors. Great Smoky Mountains welcomed almost three times as many people as Zion. Its accessible location in Tennessee and North Carolina by way of the Blue Ridge Parkway allows high numbers of visitors, making this the most visited national park year after year.

Natural disasters

Extreme weather events can cause devastation in the parks. This is obviously beyond control, but there are emergency response teams ready to help. Each park has its own preparations in place, while federal, state, and local governments also get involved.

Forest fires
Fire burned more than 10,000 acres (4,000 ha) of Acadia National Park in 1947. The Army, Air Force, Navy, and Coast Guard tackled the blaze alongside local firefighters.

Hurricanes
The hurricanes Irma and Maria destroyed much of Virgin Islands National Park in 2017. Parts of the forest lost will take years to regrow.

Tsunamis
In 2009, the National Park of American Samoa was hit by two major earthquakes and a tsunami.

Getting involved

Whatever your age, background, or interests, there are plenty of different programs available to explore the national parks in all their glory.

Girl Scouts training at Lassen Volcanic National Park

Volunteer programs
Every year more than 5,000 volunteers help out at national parks. Their jobs include collecting information, educating visitors, and maintaining trails. Best of all, you need no experience, just lots of enthusiasm for being outdoors and protecting the parks.

Junior Ranger programs
A great way to learn about the national parks from a young age is to join a Junior Ranger program (ages 5 to 13 years). Young rangers complete fun-filled activities before being rewarded with an official Junior Ranger badge and certificate.

Scout Ranger programs
The National Park Service has teamed up with the Girl and Boy Scouts of the US to create the Girl Scout and Boy Scout Ranger Program. These programs invite Scouts and Cub Scouts to join in a range of interactive projects at most national parks.

Teaching programs
Curriculum-based programs for students and teachers are available at many national parks. Teachers can accompany students on park visits to encourage their learning and spend time studying in the parks before returning to school to educate their students.

Seasonal programs
Some national parks run seasonal programs during summer and winter. They cover a wide range of enjoyable outdoor activities, including cycling in Redwood, whitewater rafting at Grand Canyon, snowshoe hiking in Rocky Mountain, and snowmobile riding in Yellowstone.

Snowshoe hike in Rocky Mountain National Park

HISTORY IN THE MAKING

Denali Museum
This museum's huge collection of over 700,000 objects and artifacts includes journals, photographs, letters, and dinosaur fossils and footprints.

Albright Visitor Center, Yellowstone
This museum charts the history of the parklands, from prehistoric times to the creation of the National Park Service.

Horseshoe Canyon, Canyonlands
The Great Gallery showcases some of the most important rock art in North America, produced by hunter-gatherers thousands of years ago.

Old Courthouse, Gateway Arch
Dating back to the 19th century, the Old Courthouse was where many enslaved Black people sued for freedom. Most famous were Dred Scott and his wife, Harriet, who got their freedom in 1857.

LOOK ONLINE

The National Park Service has its own website and downloadable app with everything you need to know.

- **www.nationalparks.org**
  This is the one-stop shop for all things national parks, including the National Park Foundation offering information about ways to support and help.

- **npmaps.com/parks**
  Grab a helpful map of any national park you are visiting here.

- **irma.nps.gov/NPSpecies**
  Find out which wildlife lives where in the national parks, so you know what to look out for, as well as endangered species that need protecting.

The National Parks: A Timeline

Protecting and preserving the most beautiful parts of North America became a focus by the 19th century. This led to the creation of the world's first national park, governed by the U.S. Department of the Interior, and within it, the National Park Service (NPS), to manage all national parks for future generations to enjoy.

1830

1832 President Andrew Jackson signs legislation to make the geothermal waters at Hot Springs in Arkansas a federal reservation and the first protected park unit. It becomes a national park in 1921.

Hot Water Cascades at Hot Springs National Park

1941 Photographer Ansel Adams is commissioned by the NPS to capture the parks on camera and also create a photographic mural for the Department of the Interior's federal building in Washington, DC.

Photo of Grand Canyon National Park by Ansel Adams

1933 President Franklin D. Roosevelt establishes the Civilian Conservation Corps (CCC), encouraging young men aged 18–25 to participate in improving North America's forests and parks. At the same time, at least 50 national monuments and military sites are moved under the NPS management.

1940 Archaeologist Louis Giddings leads pioneering excavations at a prehistoric site at Kobuk Valley National Park in northwest Alaska.

CCC members at Mount Rainier National Park

1930 Biologist George Meléndez Wright begins a detailed four-year survey of wildlife in Yosemite National Park.

1964 The introduction of the Wilderness Act protects more than nine million acres of wilderness.

1960 Almost 80 million people visit national parks this year.

1956 The NPS oversees Mission 66 projects to boost park facilities with the construction of more than 100 visitor centers.

1966 The National Historic Preservation Act is passed to protect archaeological sites. The first parks are incorporated into the National Register of Historic Places.

Rio Grande River, Big Bend National Park

1968 The Wild and Scenic Rivers Act preserves rivers, while the National Trails System Act establishes trails.

Kenai Fjords National Park

1973 The Endangered Species Act is introduced to protect endangered animals, such as the gray wolf.

1980 Biscayne and Kenai Fjords National Parks are created.

Gray wolves at Yellowstone National Park

1864 Yosemite Valley and the Mariposa Grove of giant sequoia trees become protected areas under President Abraham Lincoln. This landmark moment marks the first time governments secure land for public use and recreation.

Mariposa Grove at Yosemite National Park

1872 Yellowstone National Park makes history as the world's first national park.

Yellowstone National Park, 1870s

1892 The Sierra Club environmental organization is founded by naturalist John Muir, who becomes its first president. He convinces the U.S. government to protect Yosemite and Sequoia as national parks.

Ancestral Puebloan pottery

1906 Mesa Verde is the first national park to preserve the remnants of human history, including the biggest collection of Ancestral Puebloan homes and artifacts.

1919 Acadia in Maine becomes the first national park situated east of the Mississippi River.

Raven's Nest at Acadia National Park

1920 More than one million people visit national parks this year.

1916 The National Park Service (NPS) is established to protect and promote the 35 existing national parks and to secure the creation of more national parks offering natural and cultural value.

1917 Conservationist and entrepreneur Stephen Mather becomes the first director of the NPS, and rallies public and political support for the parks.

1910 Glacier National Park becomes the country's 10th national park, welcoming visitors to its alpine landscape and hotel accommodation that is accessible by the Great Northern Railway.

2022

1997 Former park ranger Robert Stanton is named the NPS's first Black director.

Robert Stanton

2016 Mount McKinley National Park is renamed Denali National Park to honor the Athabaskan name for the mountain. Denali means "the high one."

Mount Denali

2001 Fran P. Mainella is the first woman to serve as director of the NPS.

2020 New River Gorge becomes the newest national park. About 237 million people visit national parks in this year.

2021 Charles F. Sams III is the first Indigenous person to become director of the NPS.

New River Gorge National Park

Glossary

ALPINE Any habitat located at high altitude up in the mountains.

AMERICAN CIVIL WAR A conflict between the Northern states and the Southern states of the US that lasted from 1861 to 1865.

ARCHAEOLOGIST A person who studies ancient people and communities by excavating sites and investigating artefacts, including art, tools, and pottery.

AURORA BOREALIS Also called the Northern Lights, this is a spectacular natural light show in the most northerly skies caused by particles from the Sun hitting Earth's atmosphere.

BADLANDS Large, dry areas of land with eroded rocks, poor soil, and limited vegetation.

BASIN A bowl-shaped dip in Earth's surface caused by erosion or earthquakes.

BERING LAND BRIDGE A land crossing between North America and Asia used by ancient people more than 15,000 years ago.

CALDERA A crater that is created when the top of a volcano collapses after an eruption.

CANYON A vast valley running between two steep cliffs that often has a river flowing through it.

CLIMATE CHANGE The gradual changing of typical weather patterns on Earth as a result of natural causes or human activity.

CONIFEROUS A type of cone-bearing tree or shrub, including pine and fir trees.

CONSERVATION The protection of habitats and the plants and animals that live in them.

CORAL REEFS Hard structures in tropical waters made from the skeletons of dead marine organisms called corals.

Monarch butterfly, an endangered invertebrate

DECIDUOUS A type of tree or shrub that loses its leaves every fall.

DUNE A build-up of sand created when wind blows over a desert.

ENDANGERED SPECIES A species of animal or plant that experiences a drop in population numbers and becomes at serious risk of dying out entirely.

EROSION The process by which rock wears away in rushing wind or running water.

EXTINCT A species of animal or plant that is wiped out completely and no longer exists.

FJORD A steep-sided inlet resulting from the gradual movement of a glacier.

FOSSIL The remains of a prehistoric plant or animal preserved in Earth's crust.

FUMAROLE A hole in a volcano through which hot sulphurous gases escape.

FUNGI A group of spore-producing organisms that includes moulds and mushrooms.

GEYSER Natural hot spring that is released by pressure underground and appears on Earth's surface as a jet of water and steam.

GLACIER A huge expanse of ice and rock that moves gradually down sloping land under its own weight.

GLACIER CALVING The action of a chunk of ice breaking off a glacier and falling into the ocean as an iceberg.

GYPSUM A commonly occurring soft white crystalline mineral that resembles chalk.

HARDWOOD Strong, hard wood that comes from non-coniferous trees, including oak and ash.

Old Faithful Geyser in Yellowstone National Park

HOT SPRING Water that is naturally heated underground by volcanic activity and rushes out from Earth's surface.

ICE AGE One of many periods in Earth's history when large swathes of the planet were covered in ice and the average surface temperature was much lower than today.

ICEFIELD An enormous expanse of thick ice, usually found in one of the polar regions.

INDIGENOUS PEOPLE Communities that have lived in a specific area or place for perhaps thousands of years.

MANGROVE Tree or shrub that grows along tropical coastlines and riverbanks, with visibly tangled roots.

MARSHES Low-lying soft wetlands that are permanently waterlogged.

Aurora Borealis

Whitewater kayaking in Grand Canyon National Park

MIGRATION The seasonal movement of animals from one area to another in order to find food, better weather, or breeding grounds.

MUD POT A pool of bubbling mud typically found in volcanic areas with geothermal activity.

NOCTURNAL An animal that sleeps during the day and becomes active at night.

PADDLEBOARDING A popular watersport that involves standing on a board while using a long paddle to move along a river, lake, or sea.

PARKITECTURE A unique type of architecture that emerged in the 20th century as the National Park Service tried to construct buildings that blended with the natural surroundings.

PERMAFROST Any ground that stays below freezing point for two years or more and is usually found in the polar regions.

PETROGLYPH Pictures carved into rock by ancient people.

PICTOGRAPH Ancient pictures painted on rocks used to symbolize specific ideas.

POLYNESIA Central and southern parts of the Pacific Ocean with more than one thousand islands, such as Hawai'i and New Zealand.

PRESERVE A protected area of land that allows local communities to continue their traditions of hunting and fishing.

Petroglyph in Saguaro National Park

RAINFOREST An area of tropical woodland with towering mostly evergreen trees and heavy rainfall.

RAPIDS A fast-flowing part of a river, characterized by churning white water.

SALT FLAT A flat expanse of land topped by a layer of salt caused by water drying up.

SEDIMENTARY ROCK A type of rock created when pieces of sediment, such as sand, mud, and pebbles, form compacted deposits on Earth's surface.

SLAVERY The system of owning people as property with no rights, as well as having people work with no pay.

SPAWNING Animals, including fish and frogs, laying their eggs in water.

STALACTITES Pieces of rock that extend down from the roof of a cave and resemble icicles.

STALAGMITES Pieces of rock that grow upwards from the floor of a cave.

SUGAR PLANTATION A big area of land in a tropical region used to grow sugar.

SUSTAINABILITY Meeting the needs of present generations for food, energy, health, and housing in ways that will allow future generations to meet theirs too.

SWAMP Low-lying, boggy wetland where water collects and vegetation grows.

TECTONIC PLATE A large piece of solid rock, consisting of Earth's crust and upper mantle, that moves very slowly.

TEMPERATE Parts of the world with mild temperatures and changing seasons.

TIDES The daily rise and fall of the sea that can be seen along coastlines at high and low tide.

TUNDRA An icy area that is almost always frozen with only low-lying vegetation.

VENOMOUS Animals that can inject poisonous venom via a bite or sting.

WETLAND Any area of saturated land, including swamps, marshes, and bogs.

Venomous diamondback rattlesnake

WHITEWATER KAYAKING An adventure sport for experienced kayakers who can navigate fast-flowing and turbulent rivers.

WILDERNESS An uncultivated area of land mostly undisturbed by people.

Index

Acknowledgments

Dorling Kindersley would like to thank the following people for their help with making the book:
Kathakali Banerjee, Virien Chopra, Upamanyu Das, Alka Thakur-Hazarika, Zarak Rais, Rupa Rao, Neha Samuel, and Janashree Singha for editorial assistance; Subhashree Bharati and Simon Mumford for cartography; Shubhdeep Kaur and Deepak Negi for picture research; Mrinmoy Mazumdar and Mohd Rizwan for technical assistance; Hazel Beynon for proofreading; and Elizabeth Wise for the index.

The publishers would also like to thank the following for their kind permission to reproduce their photographs:
(Key: a-above; b-below/bottom; c-center; f-far; l-left; r-right; t-top)

Alamy Stock Photo: Agefotostock 47br, Pat & Chuck Blackley 25cla, Jennifer Booher 19tl, Cavan Images 49cl, 52bl, Ernest Cooper 52cl, Danita Delimont 29crb, 52crb, Bruce Montagne / Dembinsky Photo Associates 30br, Design Pics Inc 55c, 58bl, 60b, 61t, 61crb, Douglas Peebles Photography 64-65c, Kip Evans 48crb, Michele Falzone 43crb, Clint Farlinger 25ca, David Fleetham 45tr, Lee Foster 22cl, GRANGER - Historical Picture Archive 68cr, Jeffrey Isaac Greenberg 10+ 9cr, Steve Greenwood 32bl, 70cr, Tom Grundy 40crb, imageBROKER 5clb, 39t, Adam James 41tr, Inge Johnsson 26bl, 29tr, Morten Larsen 56bl, Fernando Lessa 54cl, Nature Picture Library 15cr, 45bl, Ilene MacDonald 18bc, Buddy Mays 56tl, Minden Pictures 16ca, 35cb, Nativestock.com / Marilyn Angel Wynn 69tr, Nature and Science 7crb, 11tl, 37bl, NPS Photo 58-59, Old Books Images 69ca, George Ostertag 4crb, International Photobank 12tl, Chuck Place 53crb, Prisma by Dukas Presseagentur GmbH 27tr, 52cr, RGB Ventures / SuperStock 60tr, Michael Nolan / robertharding 71tl, Robertharding 34cl, 37tr, RooM the Agency 42tl, Johann Schumacher 23bl, Witold Skrypczak 27clb, 29ca, 37cl, Dave Stamboulis 42-43c, C. Storz 64bl, David Stuckel 13cl, Greg Vaughn 25b, Tom Walker 59clb, 70bl, WaterFrame 8bl, Jim West 31br, 64bc, Westend61 GmbH 36t, Robert Mcgouey / Wildlife 23crb, Wonderful-Earth.net 31tr; **Alex Anderson www.alexandersonphoto.com:** 62clb; **Auburn University:** Phillip Smith 41cla; **Ed Balaun:** 20ca; **Image by Simon Barrett via https://simonandsandra.com:** 36crb; **Cherokee One;**

Feather newspaper: Scott M. Brings Plenty 14br; **Jaret Daniels, Ph.D.:** 8tr; **Photo by Jane Dodge:** 25cr; **Dreamstime.com:** Agap13 44b, Alexandrebes 14bl, Cheri Alguire 53bc, Galyna Andrushko 54clb, Rinus Baak 34crb, Jon Bilous 7tr, 17tr, Paul Brady 47cr, Harry Collins 18cl, Lane Erickson 4clb, Richard Griffin 54bc, Andrey Gudkov 5br, Hannator92 47clb, Isselee 10cl, Torsten Kuenzlen / Kuenzlen 2tl, 11clb, Francois Lariviere 4crb (Petroglyphs), Galina Lipinskaya 12cl, Luckyphotographer 37br, Mariakray 11tr, Martin Molcan 63clb, Jeffrey Ross 31l, Sekarb 54crb, Kalyan V. Srinivas 32-33c, Ievgenii Tryfonov 66cr; **Patrick Druckenmiller, University of Alaska Museum:** 59br; **Photo by Mark Egger:** 39bl; **Friends of Virgin Islands National Park:** Kayden Richards 12r; **Getty Images:** Grant Ordelheide / Aurora Photos 57br, Hal Beral 43c, Wayne Boland 30bl, Per Breiehagen 33br, Cavan Images 30crb, Mardis Coers 4t, Rachid Dahnoun 49cr, Stan Dzugan 69cl, Pavel Matejka / EyeEm 48clb, Kevin Fleming 10cra, Rene Frederick 54tl, Johnny Johnson 69cb, Photo by Mike Kline (notkalvin) 24bl, Bob Krist 10-11b, Dennis Macdonald 6ca, 26-27c, Mallardg500 17bc, Stock Montage / Contributor 27tc, Patrick Orton 53l, Donovan Reese 27crb, Ed Reschke 55crb, Manuel Romaris 3tr, 33clb, 63tr, San Francisco Chronicle / Hearst Newspapers via Getty Images 69clb, Jordan Siemens 55tr, Smith Collection / Gado / Contributor 68cl, Donald Startzell / 500px 68cb, Stephen Yelverton Photography 40-41cl, Ullstein Picture Dtl. 5tr, Peter Unger 69tl, The Washington Post 32br, © Jan Zwilling 18tl; **Getty Images / iStock:** ArendTrent 11cr, Artiste9999 36cra, Benedek 45cl, 52tl, Christiannafzger 1, 34tl, Magu Directors 46-47t, FEH 50cr, GomezDavid 56tr, Heyengel 50tl, Heath Korvola 34-35c, Mlharing 35cra, John Morrison 32cra, 68br, Pgiam 48tr, VisualCommunications 63br, Wander Photography 68crb; **Thomas Gill:** 20-21bc, 21crb; **Courtesy of Grand Canyon National Park Museum Collection:** 41bc (split-twig); **Inspired Imperfection:** Pictured here Natalie Bourn 27bc; **Leah Anderson for Wilderness Inquiry:** 23cl; **Joe Braun Photography (citrusmilo):** 38l; **Copyright Herbert K. Kane, LLC:** 65tl; **KDLG:** Hannah Colton 60cra; **Photo by Rob Kroenert:** 62c; **Las Vegas Review-Journal:** © Las Vegas Review-Journal, Inc. (2017), used with permission 38br; **Major Marine Tours:** 57c; **Matthew Bennett Bournemouth University and David Bustos National Park Service:** 29clb;

National Parks of Lake Superior Foundation: 22cr; **naturepl.com:** Karine Aigner 28cla, 28cla (bat), 28ca, Jeff Foott 42clb, Radomir Jakubowski 61cr, Nature Production 44c, Mike Read 34bl, David Welling 39cr; **Nevada Northern Railway Museum Collection:** Jason Bath 49b; **NOAA:** Don Mcleish 65bc; **NPS:** 8cr, 8-9c, 11crb, 13b, 16-17c, 21bc, 22tl, 23tr, 26tl, 34br, 36bl, 39bc, 56cr, Kim Acker 25tr, Daniel Chailloux & Peter Bosted 28tl, Emily Brouwer Photo 54cr, Gavin Emmons 45crb, Jacob W. Frank 5cl, S. Geiger 65tr, Eric Hope 41bc, HOSP 2 24cra, Matt Johnson 9br, Photo from Mammoth Cave National Park Collection 16clb, Trixine Peart 67cla, Brady Richards 30cl, Arrye Rosser 21cra, A. Schonlau 67bl, Jonathan Shafer 5tl; **Olympic Peninsula Visitor Bureau:** 55b; **Picture from Alaskan Bush Pilot, Stories by Parajumpers - Leighan Falley:** 59tr; **Aaron Peterson:** 22b; **Todd Pierson:** 2tr, 15cl; **Polaris Images:** Michael Maloney / San Francisco Chronicle / Polaris 50-51b; **Chrissy McClarren & Andy Reago:** 19cra; **Riverboats at the Gateway Arch:** 24cb; **Robert Harding Picture Library:** Harrison Shull 17clb; **CS Rogers:** 12clb; **Dave Rogers:** 30cra; **National Park of American Samoa:** 62bl, 62-63c; **Science Source:** Images & Volcans 57bl; **Sean Ryan Photography:** 4cb, 49tr; **Shutterstock.com:** All Stock Photos 24t, Galyna Andrushko 38c, Noah Berger / AP 48cl, Sekar B 57cra, Edward Bonebrake 69br, Trent Carmichael 14-15t, Cindylindowphotography 43bc, 71bl, Tomasz Czadowski 17cr, Deep Desert Photography 42crb, Gerry Matthews 44tl, MintImages 28-29b, Bram Reusen 68tr, Andrew S 51crb, William Warner 20tr, 70tc; **Tom Spinker:** 46bl; **Eliot Stein:** 55cra; **Jim Strain:** 21tl; **Photo by Thomas M. Strom:** 9tr; **SuperStock:** Fred Hirschmann 60cl; **Swain County Chamber of Commerce/Swain County TDA:** 15clb; **Elena Tudor:** 13tr; **University of Maine:** 18bl (Bonnie); **USFWS:** 13cr; **Timothy Valentine:** 18-19br; **Ethan Welty:** 56br; **Yosemite Conservancy:** Aline Allen 51tl, Keith S. Walklet 51tc

All other images © Dorling Kindersley